❧

# God's World
## and
## Our Place in It

Fulton J. Sheen

# God's World
## and
# Our Place in It

SOPHIA INSTITUTE PRESS®
Manchester, New Hampshire

*God's World and Our Place in It* was originally published as *The Moral Universe: A Preface to Christian Living* (Milwaukee: The Bruce Publishing Company, 1936). This 2003 edition by Sophia Institute Press® contains minor editorial revisions to the original text.

Sophia Institute Press®
Box 5284, Manchester, NH 03108
1-800-888-9344
www.sophiainstitute.com

*Nihil obstat:* H. B. Ries, *Censor Librorum*
*Imprimatur:* Samuel A. Stritch, Archbishop of Milwaukee
March 30, 1936

**Library of Congress Cataloging-in-Publication Data**

Sheen, Fulton J. (Fulton John), 1895-1979.
   God's world and our place in it / Fulton J. Sheen.
      p. cm.
   Rev. ed. of: The moral universe. 1936.
   ISBN 1-928832-78-4 (pbk. : alk. paper)
   1. Christian ethics — Catholic authors.  I. Sheen, Fulton J.
      (Fulton John), 1895-1979. Moral universe. II. Title.
BJ1249 .S425 2003
241'.042 — dc21                                            2002153437

03 04 05 06 07 08 10 9 8 7 6 5 4 3 2 1

*Dedicated to
the Blessed Mother
in token of
love and gratitude*

# Contents

⚛

❧

God's World
and
Our Place in It

Editor's note: The biblical quotations in the following pages are taken from the Douay-Rheims edition of the Old and New Testaments. Where applicable, quotations have been cross-referenced with the differing names and enumeration in the Revised Standard Version, using the following symbol: (RSV =).

Chapter One

# God dwells in humility in His world

❧

Every artist has the feeling of being at home in his studio, every patriot at home in his own country, and every man at home in his house. One should therefore expect that the Creator would be at home in His own creation, and that God would be at home in the world He had made. And yet the most startling fact of human history is that when God came to earth, He was homeless at home. "He came unto His own, and His own received Him not."[1] Ere yet the great portals of the flesh swung open, Mary and Joseph sought in vain for a place where might be born the One to whom the heavens and earth belonged. And so, when human history shall have written its last word in the scrolls of time, the saddest line of all will be "There was no room in the inn."[2]

There was room in the inn for those who bore on their breasts the screaming eagles of Rome; there was room for the daughters of the rich merchants of the East; there was room for all clothed in fine purple and soft garments; there was room for everyone — except the foster-father and the mother of the One who was to bring redemption to the world.

[1] John 1:11.
[2] Luke 2:7.

And so, away from the inn and out to the stable they had to go, to a crude cave into which shepherds drove their flocks in storms. In that little haven, with manger beasts as companions, and at a central point between the three great civilizations of Memphis, Athens, and Rome, something happened — the only thing in the world that ever happened and mattered. That which happened was nothing less than Heaven being found on the earth as the cry of a God cried out in the cry of a Child.

A startling paradox indeed: When God came to earth, there was no room in the inn, but there was room in the stable. What lesson is hidden behind the inn and the stable?

What is an inn, but the gathering-place of public opinion, the focal point of the world's moods, the residence of the worldly, the rallying place of the fashionable and those who count in the management of the world's affairs? What is a stable, but the place of outcasts, the refuge of beasts, and the shelter of the valueless, and therefore the symbol of those who in the eyes of public opinion do not count, and hence may be ignored as of no great value or moment? Anyone in the world would have expected to have found Divinity in an inn, but no one would have expected to have found it in a stable. Divinity, therefore, is always where you least expect to find it.

If, in those days, the stars of the heavens by some magic touch had folded themselves together as silver words and announced the birth of the Expected of the Nations, where would the world have gone in search of Him?

The world would have searched for the Babe in some palace by the Tiber, or in some gilded house of Athens, or in some inn of a great city where gathered the rich, the mighty, and the powerful ones of earth. They would not have been the least surprised to have found the newborn King of kings stretched out on a cradle of gold and surrounded by kings and philosophers paying to Him their tribute and obeisance.

But they would have been surprised to have discovered Him in a manger, laid on coarse straw and warmed by the breath of oxen, as if in atonement for the coldness of the hearts of men. No one would have expected that the One whose fingers could stop the turning of Arcturus would be smaller than the head of an ox; that He who could hurl the ball of fire into the heavens would one day be warmed by the breath of beasts; that He who could make a canopy of stars would be shielded from a stormy sky by the roof of a stable; or that He who made the earth as His future home would be homeless at home. No one would have expected to find Divinity in such a condition; but that is because Divinity is always where you least expect to find it.

⚜

### The world still doesn't know where to find God

I wonder if that is not the reason why the modern world misses the discovery of Divinity. There is no doubt that it is seeking Divinity if for no other reason than because it feels its own insufficiency and craves a God who will bring pardon for its sins and healing oil for its wounds. It seeks a Divinity who will deliver it from the terrible restlessness and emptiness of life. But where does it seek that Divinity? It seeks it in the inns where gather the publicized, the propagandized, the popular, and the modern.

The modern world looks for Divinity and the solution of its ills in the Superman of H. G. Wells, in the Humanism of Irving Babbitt, in the Sexualism of Sigmund Freud, in the Cynicism of Bertrand Russell, in the naturalism of modern religion, in the book of the month, in the reinterpreted Christ, in the new morals, in the new psychology, in the new science; but in none of these "inns" is Divinity to be found. As it was not in the inn in the first century, so it shall not be found in the inn of the current century, for what is true of the first day is true of our own: Divinity is always where you least expect to find It.

Suppose now that it was suggested to the modern world that the Divinity it seeks is to be found in the Church; suppose that it was hinted to all who are seeking for Divinity that the truth it craves is to be found only in the Vicar of Christ, who, as another Peter, articulates the mind of Christ; that the Divine Life for which it yearns is to be found only in the seven-branched fountain of the sacraments; that the pardon it begs drops from an uplifted hand in the confessional; that only in the Church's attitude toward marriage can our national fabric be preserved; and only in the Church's morality can personal virtue be regained.

Suppose that the modern world today was told that Bethlehem continued to our own day — that, by some great miracle of God's love, the stable is now the tabernacle; the manger is now the ciborium; the straw is now the altar flowers; the swaddling bands are now the white species of bread — and that the Body and Blood, Soul and Divinity of Christ is living among us in that tabernacle just as really and truly as in the crib.

Suppose, I say, that such a startling declaration was made to our day and age — and such a statement is just as true as it is startling — what would be the answer of the modern world? It would say, "That is absurd. The Church is antiquated, unmodern, behind the times; she is ignored by all the great universities of our land; her dogmas are myths; her morals, passé; her belief in the Real Presence of Christ on the altar, impossible. Why would our Lord ever live under the species of bread? Why should truth be sought in that which the world ignores? No one today ever thinks of going to the Church in search of Divinity."

But that is just exactly what the world thought in the first century. No one ever thought of going to a stable in search of the truth and life of the Son of God. But that is most likely where it is to be found, for Divinity is always where you least expect to find it.

The world has always missed Divinity, either because it has sought it in the wrong places, or because it has ignored the wrong things. It has sought Divinity in power, in popularity, in progress, in science; it has ignored the possibility of ever finding it in simplicity, in the unexpected, in defeat, and in frailty. And yet the sign of Divinity will always be the sign of seeming weakness: "This shall be to you a sign: a Babe wrapped in swaddling clothes, lying in a manger."[3] The world has always sought Divinity in the power of a Babel, but never in the weakness of a Bethlehem. It has searched for it in the inns of popular opinion, but never in the stable of the ignored. It has looked for it in the cradles of gold, but never in the cribs of straw — always in power, but never in weakness.

&#8667;

*We must seek God in weakness*

But Divinity came to earthly life in the form of a helpless Babe and left it in the form of a helpless Man. If God, therefore, is to be found by us, He must be sought in weakness and defeat, but a weakness under which there is power, and a defeat after which there is victory.

God will be found only by those who sing the hymn of the conquered and search the forgotten stables and scan the ignoble crosses. This great lesson of the Incarnation is to be remembered as the great drama of Christian morality is unfolded.

[3] Cf. Luke 2:12.

# God's World and Our Place in It

In the following chapters will be treated such old themes as God as the ground of morality, the necessity of mortification, the beauty of a retired life, the sanctity of marriage, the fact of sin, the need of Redemption, future judgment, the existence of Hell, the joy of defeat — all the pillars of the Christian moral edifice, but now so long forgotten as to be new. These are all homeless truths, for the inns of the modern world ignore them; all homeless truths because there are few who take them to heart; all homeless maxims because they are welcomed only by those whom the world ignores; all homeless gifts like the Babe of Bethlehem. The world certainly does not expect to find Divinity in such a homeless moral — but Divinity is always where you least expect to find it, and only where He was homeless are you and I at home.

*This world is wild as an old wive's tale,*
*And strange the plain things are,*
*The earth is enough and the air is enough*
*For our wonder and our war.*

*But our rest is as far as the fire drake swings*
*And our peace is put in impossible things*
*Where clash and thunder unthinkable wings*
*Round an incredible star.*

*To an open house in the evening,*
*Home shall all men come,*
*To an older place than Eden*
*And a taller town than Rome.*

*To the end of the way of the wandering star,*
*To the things that cannot be and that are,*
*To the place where God was homeless*
*And all men are at home.*

# God dwells in humility in His world

*A Child in a Foul Stable*
*Where wild beasts feed and foam*
*Only where He was homeless*
*Are you and I at home.*[4]

<hr />

[4]  From *Collected Poems*, by G. K. Chesterton.

Chapter Two

✣

# Our conscience
# directs all our actions

⸎

Modern science has explored the whole surface of the earth, made the sea reveal the secrets of its depths, the sun tell the story of its wanderings, and the stars the mystery of their light — but all this exploration is external. Modern man has done little to explore that region which is nearest to him, and yet most unknown — namely, the depths of his own conscience.

What is conscience? Conscience is an interior government, exercising the same functions as all human government — namely, legislative, executive, and judicial. It has its Congress, its President, and its Supreme Court: it makes its laws, it witnesses our actions in relation to the laws, and finally it judges us.

First of all, conscience legislates. One needs only to live to know that there is in each of us an interior Sinai, from which is promulgated amid the thunder and lightning of daily life, a law telling us to do good and avoid evil. That interior voice fills us with a sense of responsibility, reminding us, not that we *must* do certain things, but that we *ought* to do certain things, for the difference between a machine and a man is the difference between *must* and *ought*.

Without even being consulted, conscience plays its legislative role, pronouncing some actions to be in themselves evil and unjust, and others in themselves moral and good. Hence, when citizens fail to see a relationship existing between a human law and the law of their own conscience, they feel that they are free to disobey, and their justifying cry is "My conscience tells me it is wrong."

Secondly, conscience not only is legislative, in the sense that it lays down a law, but it is also executive, in the sense that it witnesses the application of the law to actions. An imperfect, but helpful, analogy is to be found in our own government. Congress passes a law; then the President witnesses and approves it, thus applying the law to the lives of citizens.

In like manner, conscience executes laws in the sense that it witnesses the fidelity of our actions to the law. Aided by memory, it tells us the value of our actions, tells us if we were total masters of ourselves, how much passion, environment, force, and fury influence us, and whether our consequences were foreseen or unforeseen. It shows us, as in a mirror, the footsteps of all our actions; points its finger at the vestiges of our decisions; comes to us as a true witness and says, "I was there. I saw you do it. You had such and such an intention."

In the administration of human justice, the law can call together only those witnesses who have known me externally, but conscience as a witness summons not only those who saw me, but summons *me*, who knows myself. And whether I like it or not, I cannot lie to what it witnesses against me.

Finally, conscience not only lays down laws, not only witnesses my obedience or disobedience to them, but also judges me accordingly. The breast of every man bears a silent court of justice. Conscience is the judge, sitting in judgment, handing down decisions with such authority as to admit of no appeal, for no one can appeal a judgment that he brings against himself. That is why there gather about the bar of conscience all the feelings and emotions associated with right and wrong: joy and sorrow, peace and remorse, self-approval and fear, praise and blame. If I do wrong, it fills me with a sense of guilt from which there is no escape, for if the inmost sanctuary of my being is assaulted by the stern voice of this judge, I am driven out of myself by myself. Whence, then, can I fly but to myself, with the sickening sense of guilt, remorse, and disgrace, which is the very hell of the soul?

If, on the contrary, conscience approves my action, there settles upon me, like the quiet of an evening dew, the joy that is a stranger to the passing pleasures of sense. The world may call me guilty, its courts may judge me a criminal, its irons may weigh down my flesh and bones like deep-sea anchors, but my soul builds a paradise within, against the raging opposition without, and floods it with an interior peace which the world cannot give and which the insults of the world cannot take from me.

> *He that has light within his own clear breast*
> *May sit in the center, and enjoy bright day;*
> *But he that hides a dark soul and foul thoughts*
> *Benighted walks under midday sun —*
> *Himself in his own dungeon.*

*Conscience points to God's existence*

Thus it is that by turning the searchlight into the hidden recesses, I find that my conscience reveals itself as making laws, witnessing my obedience to them, and finally as passing on them judgments of praise and blame, innocence and guilt. Manifestly, this triple role, upon the model of which all human government is based, must have a reason for its order.

But where to seek it?

# God's World and Our Place in It

If a normal intelligence, looking out upon the order of the heavens and the marvelous harmony of its brotherhood of orbs, passing by one another without a hitch or a halt, reasons back to a Mind behind the universe, why, too, should one, by looking into the world of conscience with its laws and commands, its interlacings of counsels and precepts, not reason back to some great Moral Governor as its source, which we call God? Since the external nature of the heavens is orderly and harmonious, I cannot suppose that the moral law within my breast is disorderly and chaotic. If there could never be a universe without a Mind, how could there ever be a law without a Lawmaker?

First of all, what is the source of the legislative role of my conscience which bids me to do good and avoid evil, but which does not make things right or wrong any more than the eye makes color red or white? It merely lays down the law, thus betraying that it is an intermediary between someone else and me. This law is certainly not of my own making, nor does it come from society.

It does not come from myself, for no one can be his own legislator and a superior to himself. Furthermore, if the law of conscience were of my own making, I could unmake it, but I cannot do this, for it comes to me in defiance of my own will. When my will is set against hearing it, or even obeying it, it comes as a delegate with absolute right to rule over me. This means that I did not make it, but that I am only free to obey it or to disobey it.

Neither does it come from society, for society is merely an interpreter of the law of conscience and not its author. Human laws may sanction it and elaborate it, but they do not create it. The approval or disapproval of society did not make the right and wrong of my conscience, because sometimes conscience bids us to flout the laws of society, when they are inimical to the laws of God, as was the case with the martyrs who died for the Faith. Furthermore, every decent man and woman on the face of the earth knows full well there are certain things that should not be done, even if he or she were the only person on earth, and that right is right if nobody is right, and wrong is wrong if everybody is wrong.

If, therefore, the voice of that interior Sinai of conscience is neither from me nor from society, and if it is universal in its whisperings and articulations, so that no moral creature can wholly shake it off, it must be that behind this law there is a Lawmaker, and behind this voice there is a Person, and behind this command a Power, which we call God, who has sealed upon every man coming into the world the light that slays darkness and illumines souls in the paths that lead to the land of peace and the homeland of the children of liberty.

Secondly, what is the source of the executive power of my conscience? I realize that my conscience is a witness in a courtroom — something, when I am guilty, that comes to me with a "thousand several tongues, and every tongue brings in a different tale, and every tale condemns me as a villain."[5]

Who is this witness within me who takes the stand and turns state's evidence against me? Who is this witness who cannot be bought by gold, nor crushed by threats, nor won by praise? Who is this great executive who accepts no excuse, but signs the law made by conscience and applies its action? Who is this witness who is always upholding the cause of truth and righteousness?

In vain do I say that it comes from society, for conscience sometimes denies the testimony of society and calls me vicious when society calls me virtuous. In vain do I say that it comes from myself, for if it did, I could make it testify in my defense, like some alienists who witness to the truth of the side which hires them.

[5]   William Shakespeare, *King Richard III*, Act 5, scene 3.

# God's World and Our Place in It

Since, therefore, my conscience witnesses constantly to truth and righteousness, and since this fidelity is not of my own making, nor the making of society, it must therefore be that behind this truth and righteousness there is a piety and a holiness; and since piety and holiness can belong only to a person, I must conclude that such a holy person who witnesses my actions is in some way the same God as the power who laid down the law of my conscience and now urges me to be faithful unto it even for eternity.

Thirdly, the sentiments of praise and blame that follow upon the judgment of conscience are meaningless unless our actions are an offense against a personal being. If men thought that they were responsible for their evil thoughts and words and actions to no one higher than themselves or their fellows, it is inconceivable that the consciousness of guilt and the fear of punishment would have been what both heart and experience testify them to be. Prayers and penances, sacrifices and atonements would never have prevailed so widely if there were no underlying sense of the existence of One before whom we are responsible and whose wrath must be turned aside. Were there no God to fear, the criminal would never be so alive to his guilt and so haunted and appalled by the fear of a judgment and a justice more terrible than that of men.

As Cardinal Newman has put it:

Inanimate things cannot stir our affections; they are correlative with persons. If, as is the case, we feel responsibility, are ashamed, are frightened, at transgressing the voice of conscience, this implies that there is One to whom we are responsible, before whom we are ashamed, whose claims upon us we fear. If on doing wrong, we feel the same tearful, broken-hearted sorrow which overwhelms us on hurting a mother; if, on doing right, we enjoy the same serenity of mind, the same soothing, satisfactory delight which follows on one receiving praise from a father — we certainly have within us the image of some person to whom our love and veneration look, in whose smile we find our happiness, for whom we yearn, toward whom we direct our pleadings, in whose anger we are troubled and waste away. If the cause of these emotions does not belong to this visible world, the object to which his perception is directed must be supernatural and divine; and thus the phenomena of conscience, as a dictate avails to impress the imagination with the picture of a Supreme Governor, a Judge, holy, just, powerful, all-seeing, retributive.

Thus, an examination of my conscience and its triple role forces me to conclude that, just as the eye corresponds to things visible, the ear to things audible, reason to things intelligible, so, too, the law of my conscience must correspond to a power that legislates, the witness of my conscience must correspond to a righteousness that executes, and the praise and blame of my conscience must correspond to a justice that judges.

And since power, righteousness, and justice correspond to the essential attributes of a person, I must conclude that that personal power is intelligent in order to make laws; that that personal righteousness is all-knowing in order to have a perfect insight into moral character; and that that personal justice is supreme in order to pass sentences after His judgments.

And that wise Power, all-knowing Righteousness, and supreme Justice, before whom I kneel in sorrow even when I have not broken a single law of the land, and confess with deep anguish of soul, "Against Thee have I sinned"; that Power who calls me away from the sin that corrodes even when it does not glare, and undermines even when it does not crush; that Righteousness who has implanted a spiritual law of gravitation within me to draw me away from the earth, beyond the stars to Himself as the source of life and truth and love; that Justice who has implanted in me a spark that the wings of angels fan into a flame of everlasting happiness is the Power, the Righteousness, and the Justice which is God.

Chapter Three

✤

# In God's world,
# man is free

If God is power, love, and justice, why did He create this kind of world? If He is powerful, why does He permit evil? If He is love, why does He tolerate hate? If He is justice, why does He allow unrighteousness? These questions, I suppose, have been asked by everyone whose eyes have ever seen and whose minds have ever known the terrible contrast between the sin of the world and the goodness of God.

To answer correctly the question of why God made this kind of world, it is important, first of all, to remember that this is not the only kind of world that God could have made. He might have created ten thousand other kinds of worlds, in which there never would have been struggle, pain, or sacrifice. But this is the best possible kind that God could have made for the purpose He has in mind. An artist is to be judged, not so much by the masterpiece he produces, as by the purpose he had in mind in creating the masterpiece. An architect is not to be judged a poor architect because he designs a birdhouse instead of a cathedral, for his intention may have been only to construct a haven for the winged creatures of God instead of a dwelling for God Himself. In like manner, God must not be judged only by this particular kind of world that He created, but also by the intention and will He had in making it.

This brings us to the other question: What purpose did God have in mind in making this kind of world?

The answer is very simply that God intended to construct a moral universe. He willed from all eternity to build a stage on which characters would emerge. He might, of course, have made a world without morality, without virtue, without character — a world in which each and every one of us would sprout virtues as an acorn sprouts an oak, or a world in which each of us would become saints with the same inexorable necessity that the chariot of the sun mounts the morning sky, or the rain falls to embrace the earth. God might have made us all like so many sticks and stones, in which we would be guided by the same necessity by which fire is hot and ice is cold.

God might have done this, but He did not. And He did not because He willed a moral universe in order that, by the right use of the gift of freedom, characters might emerge. What does God care for things, piled into the infinity of space, even though they be diamonds, for if all the orbits of heaven were so many jewels glittering like the sun, what would their external but necessarily undisturbed balance mean to Him in comparison with a single character, which could weave the skeins of an apparently wrecked and ruined life into the beautiful tapestry of saintliness and holiness? The choice before God in creating the world lay between creating a purely mechanical universe, peopled by mere automatons, and creating a world of pure spiritual beings, for whom the choice of good and evil was, at any rate, a possibility.

⚓

*In a moral universe, man must be free*
Suppose, now, it be granted that God chose to make a moral universe, or one in which characters would emerge. What condition

would have to be fulfilled in order to make morality possible? If God chose to make a moral universe, He had to make man free; that is, endow him with the power to say yes and no, and to be captain and master of his own fate and destiny.

Morality implies responsibility and duty, but these can exist only on condition of freedom. Stones have no morals, because they are not free. We do not praise iron because it becomes heated by fire, nor do we condemn ice because it is melted by heat. Praise and blame can be bestowed only on those who are masters of their own will. It is only the man who has the possibility of saying no who can have so much charm in his heart when he says yes.

Take this quality of freedom away from a man, and it is no more possible for him to be virtuous than it is for the blade of grass that we tread beneath our feet. Take freedom away from life, and there would be no more reason to honor the fortitude of the martyrs who offered their bodies as incense in testimony of their Faith than to honor the flames that kindled their pyres. Take away freedom, and where would be the concern over how children will mold their lives and write their eternal destiny in the invisible ink of their free choice? Take away freedom, which gives life the interest of an everlasting plot, and with how little care would we watch the curtain rise, and with what feeble regret would we watch the drop scene fall.

Is it any impeachment of God that He has chosen not to reign over an empire of chemicals? If, therefore, God has deliberately chosen a kind of empire to be ruled not by force, but by freedom, and if we find His subjects able to act against His will, as stars and atoms cannot, does this not prove that He has possibly given to them the chance of breaking allegiance, in order that there may be meaning and glory in that allegiance when they freely choose to give it?

❧
*Man's freedom allows for evil*

We have said that God chose to make a moral universe, and secondly, that He could make a moral universe only on condition that He made man free. This being so, we have an answer to the question "Why does God permit evil?"

The possibility of evil is in some way bound up with the freedom of man. Since man was free to love, he was free to hate; since he was free to obey, he was free to rebel; since he was free enough to be praised for his goodness, he was free enough to be blamed for his badness.

Virtue, in this present concrete order, is possible only in those spheres in which it is possible to be vicious; sacrifice is possible only in those levels in which it is possible to be selfish; redemption is possible only in those realms where it is possible to be enslaved. The world has no heroes except in those battles where every hero might have been a coward; the nation has no patriots except in those causes where each patriot might have been a traitor; the Church has no saints except in those realms where each heart might have been a devil. Triumphal arches are reared only to men who succeeded, but who might have failed in the trying; niches are filled only by the statues of those who might have transgressed, but did not; monuments are erected only to the memory of those who might have turned back, and yet pushed on.

Take the danger and doubt away from life, and where would be the heroism and faith? Let there be no sorrow by night, no malady by day, and where would be kindness and sacrifice? No watchful love hovers over the invulnerable; no crown of merit ever rests suspended over those who do not fight; they might all go forth to battle and enterprise alone, and be forgotten, followed by no musing fancy that is flushed with their triumph, or anguished with their fall. A world without contingency could have no hero and no saint.

There is no epic of the certainties, and no lyric without the suspense of sorrow and the sigh of fear, and there can be no morality in the present order without the possibility of evil, and no saints without the possibility of each one becoming a Judas.

If, then, the possibility of evil is in some way involved in human freedom, one can immediately see the absurdity of condemning God for allowing evil to continue. How many there are who say, "If I were God, I would immediately destroy all injustices and evils." To ask this, however, is to ask that God contradict Himself: you ask that God should create a thing free to choose between good and evil, and yet oblige that thing to choose good. To ask that God should create a man free to choose between justice and injustice, and yet oblige him always to choose justice and never be unjust, is to ask an absurdity. Just as it is impossible in the very nature of things for God to create me and not to create me, to make me exist and not exist at the same time, so it is impossible in the nature of things for God to make me free and yet make me a slave. God cannot do anything that would contradict His nature, not in the sense that He is bound by anything outside Himself, but because His nature is justice itself.

And so those who would blame God for allowing man freedom to go on hindering and thwarting His work are like those who, seeing the blots and smudges and misspellings and grammatical errors in a student's notebook, would condemn the teacher for not snatching away the book and doing the copy himself. Just as the object of the teacher is sound education and not the production of a neat and well-written copybook, so the object of God is the development of souls and not the production of biological entities, however perfect they may be.

There, too, is the answer to those who ask, "If God knew that I would sin, why did He make me?" Very simply, insofar as I am a sinful being, God did not make me. I made myself. I am a self-creating being. God gave me power, but I am free to decide the manner of man I shall be. Hence, my success or failure is in my own hands and I am responsible for the result.

❧

### Each person must choose whether to obey God's law

Since the universe is moral, it follows that the supreme choice that lies before us is that of obeying the law of God or rebelling against it. If you choose to rebel against that law, as if you were your own, and as if Christ had never bought you with His Blood, then you must remain eternally in the congregation of the dead. Not for you will be the glory of consecrated knowledge; not for you the rich blessings of Him who turns a soul from the error of its ways; not for you the steady love of good, even if it be persecuted, or the steady scorn of evil, even if it be enthroned; but for you the frivolous insipidity of irreverent amusements — the dull and discontented mind, ignoble when with another, wretched when alone. Great deeds will be done, but you will not be at their doing; high thoughts will be uttered, but they shall awaken no echo in the seared conscience and sodden heart. Beyond you shall sweep the godlike procession of the nobly virtuous and the greatly wise, but you shall not be found among their ranks.

If you choose to offend God, successful you may be, honored you may be, rich you may be, praised by the world you may be, "broad-minded" and "progressive" you may be, alive to public opinion and to the new morals of the day you may be, but you will never know how much you have failed, as Barabbas never knew how much he failed the day of his success. But you will be dead:

dead to the life of Christ, dead to the love of God, dead to the age-less peacefulness of eternity!

If, on the contrary, you obey the laws of God and live as if you were really destined for a life beyond the grave, the battle in which the love of God gains mastery over the love of self may be fierce, and for the short time of our bodily life every tree may be a cross, every bush may be a crown of thorns, and every friend may be a Judas. Poor you may be on this earth, with no more comfort than a Carpenter once had at Nazareth; sorrowful you may be as each day brings to you a new cup of passion, filled with the bitterness of Gethsemane; solitary you may be with not even a Veronica to wipe away the salt of righteous tears; scorned and ridiculed you may be by a world of darkness that comprehends not the light; thirsty you may be as your soul, in the fire of its crucifixion, cries out for the cool draughts of a divine refreshment; a failure you may be, an unworldly dreamer, a fool, but in all the world's burnt wilderness, your food shall be the Manna from the Paradise of God, and your drink the fountain of everlasting life. But alive you shall be: alive to Christ, alive to the spirit, alive to life, alive to God — and if God is your life, who can take it from you?

Chapter Four

# We must choose between good and evil

Since God chose to make a moral universe in which, by the right of the gift of freedom, characters might emerge, this world is a battleground of the forces of good and evil. This being so, it is important to ask ourselves whether we may be disinterested in that struggle.

There are two answers to this question: one, the answer of the world; the other, the answer of our blessed Lord. The answer of the world is summed up in one word: *indifference*; the answer of our blessed Lord in the words "The kingdom of Heaven suffereth violence, and the violent bear it away."[6]

❧
### Indifference leads to the loss of our souls
In religious matters, the modern world believes in indifference. Very simply, this means it has no great loves and no great hates; no causes worth living for and no causes worth dying for. It counts its virtues by the vices from which it abstains, asks that religion be easy and pleasant, sneers the term *mystic* at those who are spiritually inclined, dislikes enthusiasm and loves benevolence, makes

[6] Matt. 11:12.

elegance the test of virtue and hygiene the test of morality, and believes that one may be too religious but never too refined. It holds that no one ever loses his soul, except for some great and foul crime, such as murder. Briefly, the indifference of the world includes no true fear of God, no fervent zeal for His honor, no deep hatred of sin, and no great concern for eternal salvation.

Such indifference has always been in the world, and our blessed Lord has warned that it shall be in it unto the end: "And as it came to pass in the days of Noah, so shall it be also in the days of the Son of Man. They did eat and drink, they married wives and were given in marriage, until the day that Noah entered the ark and the flood came and destroyed them all. Likewise as it came to pass, in the days of Lot: they did eat and drink, they bought and sold, they planted and built. And in the day that Lot went out of Sodom, it rained fire and brimstone from heaven, and destroyed them all. Even thus shall it be in the day when the Son of Man shall be revealed."[7]

It is important to remember that such indifference to our souls and the conflict of good and evil is wholly wrong. As a matter of fact, we lose our souls by the very process of not resisting the forces that pull us down. This is true in the natural order as well as in the spiritual. What is life, for example, but the sum of those forces that resist death? What is the biological principle of reversion to type but a proof of how we may lose ourselves by neglect?

Suppose a bird-fancier, through industry and skillful mating, has brought a flock of pigeons to a high degree of perfection as regards color and form. Suppose, furthermore, they were brought to a desert isle and there abandoned. After many years, the bird-fancier would return for his pigeons. He would discover that they

[7] Luke 17:26-30.

had lost the improvement that was due to his skill and knowledge, and that their highly developed colors had changed to a dull slate-gray.

What is true of the animal order, as regards reversion to type, is true also of man. Man, too, degenerates by the mere fact that he neglects. Although there is within him a spiritual principle which, like a flame, mounts upward to the heavens with God, there is also within him something that drags him down to the earth with the beasts.

Hence, man is always conscious of being a dual being: of wanting the better, but sometimes choosing the worse. This force of degeneration within him; the consequence of Original Sin, if it is not resisted by nature and grace, will eventually end in his reversion to the type Adam, or sin. Hence, the degeneration of the moral and intellectual faculties of man follows like an inexorable law upon his neglect to combat the forces that make for spiritual death.

To illustrate this principle, suppose a man had fallen from the eightieth floor of the Empire State Building. In his rapid descent, he might still be alive as he passed the twenty-fifth floor, and yet no one who saw him falling at that point would be sufficiently an optimist to believe that he would escape death, simply because the principle of death is already in him. The man had neglected to take the precautions that would prevent the principle of death from working itself out in his life, and because he neglected, he must succumb.

Or, suppose a man has taken poison. As it begins to eat its way through the gates and alleys of his body, an antidote is brought to him. In order for the poison to work out its law of death, it is not necessary that the sick man violently cast the antidote out the window or, with a blasphemy against the one who brought it, throw it on the floor. It merely suffices that he neglect to take the remedy.

So it is with the moral life of man. He loses his soul, not only by committing grave sins, but also by neglecting to respond to the grace that prevents sin and brings everlasting union with God.

What is it that dries up the wells of repentance but the neglect of meditating on the heinousness of sin? What makes devotion well-nigh impossible, but the neglect of prayer? What makes God seem so far away and so unreal, but the neglect of living in His holy presence? What is it that drags a soul down to Hell but the neglect to lift itself up to Heaven?

Let a man be solely at ease in himself, satisfied with what he is, consenting to the customs of the world, drawing in the unwholesome breath of refined evil, and letting his moral inclinations run their natural course without check or stay, and he will most surely tide onward, with an easy and gentle motion, down the broad current of eternal death, for in the language of Paul, "How shall we escape, if we neglect?"[8]

⚶

*Neglect carries a*
*penalty even in this life*

Even in this life there is a terrible penalty for neglect. That penalty is the warping and the atrophying and the dulling of those faculties which were meant to feed on the things of God. God gave us a mind to know Him, a will to love Him, and a body to serve Him. If we neglect these energies of body and soul by not lifting them up in adoration of the Father, from whom all gifts come, nature takes a terrible revenge. Something happens to us that

[8]  Heb. 2:3.

happens to the lower animals — namely, we lose the use of these faculties and also the high objects toward which they should have been directed.

There is some scientific warrant for the fact that the mole was not always blind. It chose, however, to spend its life underground and not to use its faculty of vision. Nature, as if sitting in judgment, practically said to the mole, "If you will not use the eyes I have given you, I shall strike you blind."

And so, the penalty of neglect is the surrender of even the gifts that we have. It is this lesson that our blessed Lord revealed in the parable of the talents. "And to one he gave five talents and to another two and to another one."[9] He who received the five talents gained another five. In like manner, he who received the two gained another two. "But he that had received the one, going his way, digged into the earth and hid his lord's money."[10] But when the reckoning day came, he who had received the five talents and he who had received the two talents, and had earned another five and another two, were admitted into the joy of the Lord. But he who had done nothing with the gift that had been given to him, but merely hid it in the earth, had to suffer the penalty of the forfeiture of the talent, for the Lord said, "Take ye away therefore the talent from him."[11] The deprivation was the natural consequence of his sloth.

As the arm of a man, if never called into exercise, loses its strength by degrees, and its muscles and its sinews disappear, even so the powers that God gave us, when unexercised, fail and fade from us. "For to everyone that hath shall be given and he shall

[9] Matt. 25:15.
[10] Matt. 25:18.
[11] Matt. 24:28.

abound, but for him that hath not that also which he seemeth to have shall be taken away."[12]

Our land is full of men and women who have neglected their talents, whose spiritual faculties have dried up through sheer indifference, and who now no more think of God than they think of the political situation in Timbuktu. The eternal aspirations of their souls are crushed, each inlet to Heaven is barricaded, every talent is squandered, and every faculty of the divine is so bent on things of earth as to lose all relish for those of spirit. Daily and hourly they lose their sensitivity as regards the great realm of the soul. Just as the deaf are dead to the harmonies of life, such as the sigh of a waterfall and the rhythm of poetry; just as the blind are dead to the beauties of nature, such as the colors of a rainbow and the smile of a child; so, too, these atrophied souls are dead to the sweet whisperings of the Holy Spirit and blind to the dazzling vision of Jesus in the monstrance.

It was of such souls who neglected hearing the word of God and seeing the vision of His Son that our blessed Lord spoke, when He said, "Seeing, they see not, and hearing, they hear not, neither do they understand."[13]

⚜

### We must use our faculties
### and talents to serve God

If, then, the penalty for neglect and indifference is so terrible, should we not gird up the energy of our moral nature for a struggle? The most watchful must feel as one who cannot neglect for an hour, even as the apostles in the garden. The most aspiring must

[12] Matt. 24:29.
[13] Cf. Matt. 13:14; Mark 4:12.

feel as one who aims his shaft from a strained and slackened bow. The most hopeful of eternal life must feel as one who must enter the narrow gate and travel the straight road.

Salvation is not the by-play of idle hours! When the mind is wearied of overtoiling and is cloyed with the oppressive customs of the world, it must goad itself to remember that redemption is not for those who bury their talents in napkins. Across the centuries there comes the cry for strong men who will enter into the struggle, take up their crosses, and persevere to the end.

From out of high Heaven, in thoughts of sweet inspiration and actual grace, there comes the challenge to develop and perfect the faculties God has given us, lest by our neglect and our abuse we lose their use. Hands must not be neglected, but trained to break the bread for the poor who come in the name of Christ. Feet must not be neglected, but bidden zealously, like the Man of Nazareth, to go about doing good. Eyes must not be neglected by turning them outward to the beauties of nature, but must be turned inward to the soul, where resides the beauty of the daughter of the king. Ears must not be neglected, but attuned to the delicate whisperings of the Trinity, taking up Its abode in the soul and making of the body a veritable temple of God. Hands must not be dulled, fumbling with the treasures that rust consumes and moths eat and thieves break in and steal,[14] but must be quickened to enjoy, like the Canaanite woman, the touch of the hem of the garment of God.[15]

Taste must not be neglected by eating only the meat which perishes, but refined to enjoy the Bread of Life and the Wine which germinates virgins. The sense of smell must not be neglected by

[14] Cf. Matt. 6:20.
[15] Mark 5:25-29.

dulling itself with the perfumes of Arabia, but must absorb the odor of sanctity, which emanates from every soul that has touched the rod and root of Jesse.

Finally, the heart must not be neglected by loving only the embrace of that which time steals away, but must love that "Love we fall just short of in all love and the Beauty which leaves all other beauty pain."

In a word, every fiber, every muscle, every sense, and every faculty must be used to win the eternal crown, for may it not be that all our indifference to the gifts and the graces of God in this day and age is more crucifying to our Lord than the cruel intolerance that nailed Him to a Cross?

> When Jesus came to Golgotha,
>     they hanged Him on a tree;
> They drove great nails through hands
>     and feet, and made a Calvary;
> They crowned Him with a crown of thorns,
>     red were His wounds and deep,
> For those were crude and cruel days,
>     and human flesh was cheap.
>
> When Jesus came to Birmingham,
>     they simply passed Him by.
> They would not hurt a hair of Him,
>     they only let Him die;
> For men had grown more tender, and
>     they would not give Him pain,
> They only just passed down the street,
>     and left Him in the rain.
>
> Still Jesus cried, "Forgive them, for
>     they know not what they do,"

*And still it rained the winter rain that*
  *drenched Him through and through;*
*The crowds went home and left the*
  *streets without a soul to see,*
*And Jesus crouched against a wall,*
  *and cried for Calvary.*[16]

---

[16] G. A. Studdert-Kennedy.

Chapter Five

# Attaining a higher life means dying to a lower life

⚘

It is one of the curious anomalies of present-day civilization that when man achieves greatest control over nature, he has the least control over himself. The great boast of our age is our domination of the universe: we have harnessed the waterfalls, made the wind a slave to carry us on wing of steel, and squeezed from the earth the secret of its age. Yet, despite this mastery of nature, there perhaps never was a time when man was less a master of himself. He is equipped like a veritable giant to control the forces of nature, but is as weak as a pigmy to control the forces of his passions and inclinations.

If, indeed, this life is a vale of character-making, and if it involves conflict with those forces and powers that would drag us away from our ideals, then it behooves us to realize that the truest conquest is self-conquest, that true progress may more properly consist in mastering our rampant impulses and selfish desires, than in mastering the winds and the seas. But this conquest of self cannot be attained except by a struggle that in Christian language is mortification. Mortification means dying to live for the love of God.

First of all, it means dying to live. It is a law of nature and grace that a higher life is purchased only by dying to a lower one, or that we live to the life of the spirit and the kingdom of God only by dying to this world, with its flesh and its concupiscence. Recall the tremendous emphasis that our blessed Lord placed upon this aspect of mortification — words we only rarely hear in these milk-and-water Christianities of our day:

"Amen, Amen, I say to you, unless the grain of wheat falling to the ground die, itself remaineth alone. But if it die, it bringeth forth much fruit."[17]

"Enter you in at the narrow gate, for wide is the gate and broad is the way that leadeth to destruction, and many there are who go in thereat. How narrow is the gate and straight is the way that leadeth to life: and few there are that find it."[18]

"If any man will come after me, let him deny himself, and take up his cross and follow me."[19]

"If any man come to me and hate not his father and mother and wife and children and brethren and sisters, yea, and his own life also, he cannot be my disciple."[20]

"And if thy hand scandalize thee, cut it off: it is better for thee to enter into life maimed, than having two hands to go into Hell, into unquenchable fire, where the worm dieth not, and the fire is not extinguished. And if thy foot scandalize thee, cut it off. It is better for thee to enter lame into life everlasting than having two feet to be cast into the Hell of unquenchable fire, where the worm dieth not, and the fire is not extinguished. And if thy eye scandalize thee, pluck it out. It is better for thee with one eye to enter into the kingdom of God, than having two eyes to be cast

[17] John 12:24-25.
[18] Matt. 7:13-14.
[19] Matt. 16:24.
[20] Luke 14:26.

into the Hell of fire, where the worm dieth not, and the fire is not extinguished."[21]

"The kingdom of Heaven suffereth violence, and the violent bear it away."[22]

"For whosoever will save his life shall lose it; but he that shall lose his life for my sake shall save it."[23]

These warnings sound strange to us, whose lives are molded so often on the assumption that this life is the only one we can be sure of, and hence, while we have it, we should eat, drink, and be merry, for tomorrow we die. They sometimes are dismissed with a shrug of the shoulders, as if such suggestions belonged to the past and should have no part in our modern life of ease and luxury.

The law of mortification, which consists in dying to live, is one of the fundamental laws of life and one that cannot be ignored by anyone who knows the meaning and purpose of life. As the poet has put it:

> For birth hath in itself the germ of death,
> But death hath in itself the germ of birth.
> It is the falling acorn buds the tree,
> The falling rain that bears the greenery,
> The fern-plants moulder when the ferns arise,
> For there is nothing lives but something dies,
> And there is nothing dies but something lives
> Till skies be fugitives,
> Till time, the hidden root of change, updries,
> Are Birth and Death inseparable on earth;
> For they are twain, yet one, and Death is Birth.

[21] Mark 9:42-47.

[22] Matt. 11:12.

[23] Luke 9:24.

Glance over the various levels of creation — the chemical, the plant, the animal, and the human order — and see how well verified is the law that a higher life is purchased only by death to a lower life.

Note that if the sunshine and the rain and the chemicals of the earth are ever to enjoy communion with plant life, so much as to be one with its organism and enjoy the thrill of living, they must surrender their form of existence in the lower order. If the grass of the field is to enjoy communion with the life of the animal and be so much with it that it can see, taste, touch, and smell with the animal, it must die to its lower life; this means that as grass it must be torn up from the soil by the very roots and ground between the jaws of death. For death is the condition of birth. If the sunshine and the rain, if the plants and the flowers, if the animals and the birds, if the great expanse of living things are ever to enjoy communion with a higher life of man, so much so as to become a part of his life as a thinking and loving being, they, too, must surrender their lower lives and existences and pass through the Calvary and the Gethsemane of death.

⚛

### We must die to ourselves to attain life with Christ

In like manner, if a man is ever to enter into the higher life of Christ — and man has no right to say there is no higher life than his own, any more than a rose has a right to say there is no higher life than its own — if he is ever to enjoy communion with Him, so as to have the blood of God running in his veins and the spirit of God throbbing in his soul, he must die to the lower life of the flesh. Yes, he must be born again, for unless a man is born to that life of God by a death to the lower life of nature, he cannot enter the kingdom of Heaven.

## Attaining a higher life means dying to a lower life

And hence the law of Calvary is the law of every Christian: unless there is the Cross, there will never be the Resurrection. Unless there is the defeat of Calvary, there will never be the victory of Easter. Unless there are the nails, there will never be the glorious wounds. Unless there is the garment of scorn, there will never be the robes blazing like the sun. Unless there is the crown of thorns, there will never be the halo of light. Unless there is the descent into the grave, there will never be the Ascension. For the law laid down at the beginning of time, which shall be effective until time shall be no more, is that no one shall be crowned unless he has struggled and overcome, and no one shall enjoy the life of God until he has died to his selfish self.

But in this surrender of the lower life, let it not be thought that mortification is a sign of weakness; rather, it is a sign of power. It is the will controlling itself, submitting itself to defeat at its own hands, in order to win its finest victory. It is the making of the dead self a stepping stone to better things and the conquest of self the condition of the victory that brings everlasting peace and joy with God.

Wrongly indeed do we think that our blessed Lord might have saved us in some less costly way than in emptying His Precious Blood from the chalice of His body. Oh, if He were only a teacher of humanitarian ethics, if He were only a moral reformer, then it might have sufficed for Him to show His inimitable tenderness, His heavenly purity, and His melting kindness. Then He might have sat like some Greek teachers before Him in some marketplace or on some porch, where the great minds of the world might have sought out His wisdom and His counsel.

But if He was to be more than a teacher, if He was to be the High Priest who would not make a new world but invigorate an old one, if He was to force the human conscience to stand face-to-face with the sternest sides of truth ere He disclosed His divine remedy, then, unless the existing conditions of human life were to be altered, He had to die to the ignominy of a Good Friday to live to the life of an eternal Easter. Since the servant is not above the Master, how can we expect to avoid the law of Christ?

࿇

### Love is the root of sacrifice

But mortification means not only dying to live. Its fullest meaning embraces also its inspiration, which is love, for the difference between pain and sacrifice is love. Love is the soul of sacrifice. Everything in nature testifies to this: the deer that fights for her fawn, the bird that toils for her nestlings, the spider that would die rather than drop her bag of eggs: all these know that love is not worth calling love unless it can dare and suffer for the one it loves.

That, too, is why I believe that we always speak of arrows and darts of love — something that wounds. The day that man forgets that love is identical with sacrifice, he will ask how a God of love could demand mortification and self-denial. As a matter of fact, the most intense human sufferings and the bitterest arrows of outrageous fortune become softened and sometimes sweetened when they are borne in love for another. A mother keeps vigil by the bedside of her fever-stricken child; neighbors call it sacrifice, but she calls it love. The hero rushes into lapping tongues of fire to rescue his friend; onlookers call it sacrifice, but he calls it love. The lover gives to his beloved a ring, not of tin or straw, but of diamonds and platinum; acquaintances call it sacrifice, but he calls it love. And finally, our blessed Lord empties Himself of His heavenly glory, puts on the cloak of mortality, and goes down to the horrible red death of a crucifixion; we call it sacrifice, but He calls it love: "Greater love than this no man hath: that he lay down his life for his friends."[24]

Hence, whenever and wherever there is an intense and passionate love of Christ and Him crucified, sacrifice involved in crushing anything that keeps one away from Him is not felt pain but the sweetest kind of love, for what is pain but sacrifice without love? The saint does not view sacrifice as an executioner with a sword who will take away his life, but as a yoke that is sweet and a burden that is light. The devout do not hate life because life hates them or because they have drunk of its dregs and found them bitter, but because they love God more, and in loving God more, they dislike anything that would tear Him away.

Oh, could the world but realize that the love of Christ crucified so possesses thousands and tens of thousands of souls that they would rather lose all the world and the riches thereof than one second of intimacy with Him at the foot of the Cross! Could it but sense the passionless passion and wild tranquility with which such souls each morning rush to Communion to enjoy intimate union with their changeless and understanding Friend, Jesus in the Eucharist! Could it but dimly guess how these Christ-loving hearts rejoice in carrying a cross, in order that, by sharing in His death, they might also share in His Resurrection!

Sacrifice for them is not a loss, but an exchange; not a suffering, but a dedication; not a foregoing of the enjoyable, but a conversion of passing pleasures into an eternal and unchangeable joy. Sacrifice for them is not pain, but love. Their only pain, in fact, is their inability to do more for their Beloved. Like ships, which never know the full joy and the great glory for which they are made until they are unmoored from port and given over to the

---

[24] Cf. John 15:13.

high seas and strong winds, so neither do souls know the full joy of their life until they, too, are unmoored from the port of all worldly attachments and, following the words of our blessed Lord: "launch out into the deep."[25] Like coals, conscious of their own blackness, they cast themselves into the fire of sacrifice, there to become Christlike in flaming brilliance. Like the logs of the forest, these souls, once in the consuming fire of the love of the Cross, sing their song, for the log sings its song only in the fires that consume. Possessed with the desire to be like their Christ, none of them will come down from the Calvary of this world with hands unscarred and white. They are like other Sauls made Pauls by their intense love of the Savior, and there floats up like burning incense from their fiery hearts the words "Who, then, shall separate us from the love of Christ? Shall tribulations? Or distress? Or famine? Or nakedness? Or danger? Or persecution? Or the sword? I am sure that neither death, nor life, nor angels, nor principalities, nor power, nor things present, nor things to come, nor might, nor height, nor depth, nor any other creature shall be able to separate us from the love of God, which is in Christ Jesus our Lord."[26]

The world, which begins with pleasure instead of ending with it, perhaps can never understand why such an intense love of our blessed Lord should ever make souls want to die to live, and still be happy in their death. But then, neither can the world ever understand why the only recorded time that our blessed Lord ever sang was when He went out in the black, cruel night to His death![27]

[25] Luke 5:4.

[26] Rom. 8:35, 38-39.

[27] Cf. Matt. 26:30.

Chapter Six

༕

# God calls some persons to the religious life

In a moral universe, the soul is saved, not by indifference to the conflict of good and evil, but by an act of choice in which the soul loves God above all things else. There are many ways to love God, among which two deserve special mention: one is to seek the divine love through the divine, and that is the way of the religious life; the other is to seek the divine through the human, and that is the way of Matrimony. Here I am presently concerned with the first way of those chosen souls who, like moths, leap into the flame, there to be consumed by love and yet live in it.

In order that we might understand it aright, two very important points must be borne in mind. The first is that everyone in the world is in pursuit, not of the lovely, which belongs to earth, but of love, which belongs to God. The second is that the religious does it directly through purity, so that the religious life may be defined as the pursuit of the love of God through purity.

First, every human heart in the world is on the quest of the love of God even when it seems to be loving the lovely. The first look that man bestowed on the visible universe at the beginning of time was the sad look of Genesis; Adam found no one like unto himself, and when God gave him a companion like unto himself to people his solitude, console his loneliness, and share in his embrace, he found neither in her nor in all created nature the satisfaction of his soul's desire and the full enjoyment of his ecstatic energies. From that day to this, no man has found on earth an object that completely satisfies his capacity for love.

There is something eternal involved in the quest for love, for no man could ever love anything unless he thought it eternal. The real object of love is not flesh and blood, but the ideal that flesh and blood evokes, for every human heart seeks to eternalize and infinitize the object of its love. Everyone necessarily loves the whole more than the part, and hence loves perfect Love more than any of its partial reflection in any earthly thing. That is why in human love the case has sometimes the charm that the capture has not. That is why so often the possession of an earthly love falls short of that for which we crave. That is why it may correctly be said that love is blind to limitations, blind to death because its ideal is the Perfect.

That, too, is why all the poetry of love is a cry and a moan, and the more pure it is, the more it laments. If a cry of joy interrupts this pleading, it is to celebrate the ravishing of an hour, and then to fall back into the immensity of desire.

That is why our nature is fortified by the imagination, which puts before us the thought of the beautiful, so that when earthly beauty has faded from our eyes, we might revive the ideal more beautifully still in our imagination.

The heart of man, then, is not to blame if he fills the earth with his chant of sorrow, for the real object of his love is not the lovely, which is of the kingdom of time, but the Loveliness, which is God, at whose flaming heart the sparks of our own poor hearts have been kindled.

This brings us to the essence of the religious life, which is not the indirect quest of the divine through the human, but the direct pursuit of the divine through purity. It chooses purity because it loves God more than anything else in the world. Purity is the sacristan of a soul in love with God. Oh, how little our modern world, intoxicated by the wild jargon of sex, has understood the soulful meaning of purity!

*Purity is a participation in the sublime*

There are those who mock at purity as something negative, or as a suppression of a vital urge, or as a thing cold, inert, and dead. Purity is not something negative, but something positive. Just as mercy does not mean not being cruel, or sparing people punishment, but rather something plain and positive, so, too, purity does not mean merely abstention from sexual wrong; it means participation in the sublime, something flaming and burning like the Little Flower.[28]

Purity is not a prudish or a hysterical disgust, but a reverence for God and His creation that consents to nothing incompatible with the light of holiness that shines upon us from the countenance of Jesus. Purity is not a blindness to beauty, but a vision of the beauty of God's ineffable purity, which only the clean of heart may see.

Its prototype is the purest of the pure, the Virgin Mother, who knew all and yet knew purity more; for when the angel Gabriel announced to her that she was to be the Mother of God, she replied, "How shall this be, seeing I know not man?"[29]

Purity is not a suppression or a repression, as our modern psychologists would have us believe, but a domination of the lower

[28] St. Thérèse of Lisieux (1873-1897), Carmelite nun and Doctor.
[29] Cf. Luke 1:34.

part of man, in order that the spiritual part of man might be free to busy itself with the things of God.

Just as a man, when he wishes to think clearly, shuts his eyes and closes out the disturbing factors of sense, so, too, the soul that wishes to love God wholly and entirely cuts itself away from all the pleasures of lesser loves, for why should it trouble itself with the drop of earthly love, when it can have the ocean of Infinite Love? The pure soul feels that it can very well get along without the pleasures of the flesh, but it cannot get along without the pleasures of the spirit, and so it exchanges one for the other, and that is the vow of chastity.

Purity is not abstention from passion, but the passionless passion whose fires burn not inward but upward, and whose fuel is not the flesh, but the spirit, which makes of a Magdalene a penitent and of an Augustine[30] a saint. Purity is something that revels in the preciousness of the unopened bud, and to those modern minds who would make it something frozen and sterile, there should be the memory that at the heart of love's reddest rose may reign the whitest purity. From every pure heart there goes to God the prayer:

> *Do Thou with Thy protecting hand*
> *Shelter the flame Thy breath has fanned;*
> *Let my heart's reddest glow*
> *Be, but as sun-flushed snow.*
>
> *And if they say that snow is cold,*
> *O, Chastity, must they be told*
> *The hand that's chafed with snow*
> *Takes a redoubled glow?*

[30] St. Augustine (354-430), Bishop of Hippo.

*That extreme cold like heat doth sear?*
*O to this heart of love draw near,*
*And feel how scorching rise*
*Its white-cold purities!*[31]

*God still calls souls to lives of purity*

Such is in brief the religious life of consecrated souls: the pursuit of God through purity. Although many minds are willing to concede that the real goal of the human heart is God, they are not willing to admit that one should seek it directly, and hence they raise a mild protest against the young man and woman who leave the lights and glamours of the world in the full bloom and blossom of life for the shades and shadows of the Cross where saints are made. They can understand why a human heart would weave the tendrils of its affection around a passing love, but they cannot understand why those tendrils should be rooted in a love that is eternal. They can understand why youth would love the lovely, but they cannot understand why it would love Love. They quickly comprehend why affection should be directed toward an object that age corrodes and death separates, but they cannot grasp the meaning of an affection that death makes more intimate and present. They can understand why the human heart should love the spark, but they cannot understand why it should love the Flame!

But, why should there not be hearts in the world like St. Agnes, who could say before her martyrdom when an earthly love was presented to her: "The kingdom of the world and every ornament thereof have I scorned for the love of Jesus Christ, my Lord,

---

[31] Francis Thompson.

whom I have seen and loved, in whom I have believed and who is my love's choice"? Why should there not be young men and women who would put their whole selves at the disposal of God? For the value of every gift is enhanced if it exists solely for the one to whom it is given, fulfills no other purpose, and remains unshared. Why should there not be hearts so much in love with God that they would build walls around themselves, not to keep themselves in, but to keep the world out? Why should there not be Marys and Magdalenes at the foot of the Crucifix of the twentieth century as well as at the foot of the Cross of the first? Why should there not be hearts whose first love is their last love, which is the love of God?

Why should there not be roses in God's garden? In an earthly garden is an earthly rose that has its own father and mother, brothers and sisters, hopes and aspirations for the future, its own joys and sorrows, its own laughter when there is sunshine, and its own tears when there is dew. Out into the garden comes a human hand that plucks the rose and destroys its life. The rose has a life and a right to live that life, and yet no injustice is done or murder committed, for the hand of man is above the rose in dignity and worth and may use the rose for his own sweet purposes.

In the human family is a human rose with its own real father and mother, brothers and sisters, hopes and aspirations its own real laughter, and its own real tears. From out of the high heavens there comes the hand of the Everlasting Gardener, who plucks up the human rose and destroys its life, insofar as its human environment is concerned, for that young man or woman has a human life and the right to live it. But there is no injustice done or murder committed, for as the hand of man is above the earthly rose, so the hand of God is above the human soul, and God may use it to His own sweet purposes, and God's purposes are always sweet.

But it may be asked, what benefit accrues to the poor rose that is plucked from the earthly garden? It is put into a crystal vase; refreshing waters are poured on it from day to day; it is touched by human hands; it may even be pressed to human lips and, like another John, may be privileged to tabernacle its crimson head upon the breast of the eucharistic Emmanuel.[32] Its earthly life is shortened, yes. But what a beautiful life it now begins to lead with man!

In like manner, when God plucks the young human heart from the garden of the human family, it is placed in the crystal vase of His Church; refreshing waters of sanctifying grace are poured on it from day to day; it is touched by the hands of the saints and the Mother of God and is pressed in daily communion to the Heart of Christ. Its human life is shortened, yes. But what a beautiful life it now begins to lead with God!

---

[32] John 13:23.

Chapter Seven

⁂

# God calls some
# persons to marriage

❧

The birth to a higher life of God is achieved only by discipline. In-dividual discipline at its highest peak is the religious life. Social dis-cipline in its most general form is matrimony, although there are few who think of it as such. It is a discipline because it demands of both husband and wife loyalty, fidelity, and sacrifice, through sick-ness and health, joy and sorrow, poverty and affluence, until death do them part. Everyone knows that the Church takes most seri-ously the words of our blessed Lord: "What therefore God hath joined together, let no man put asunder,"[33] but there are few who know why she is so insistent on the sanctity of the marriage bond. She has two reasons for such emphasis: one drawn from the natural order and the other from the supernatural order.

❧
*The raising of children calls*
*for the permanence of marriage*
In the natural order, love is permanent and abiding. In the lan-guage of love, there are only two thoughts: *you alone* and *always*. In the hieroglyphics of love, there is only one symbol: two hearts

[33] Matt. 19:6.

cut and interlocked in something stable and permanent, like an oak tree. In the history of love, there is only one supreme devotion: the love of offspring.

It is a well-known, observable fact that higher animals require a much longer period of parental care than lower animals do; the lower animals may therefore desert their offspring immediately after birth. But with a human father and mother, the situation is quite different. The child has to be cared for, not only physically, but mentally as well. The more things there are for the child to learn, the longer the child must remain in the natural school for learning them, and the longer his teachers must postpone the dissolution of their partnership.

In vain does one say that the function of teaching can be fulfilled adequately by the state, for the state cannot be nurse in every nursery, nor the government the governess in every playroom. There is only one place where the human tradition can be developed, and that is the home: there are only two persons who can love those whom the state does not think worth loving, and they are the father and mother. The moment we realize the child can attain the full development of heart and mind and soul only through the ministrations of those who love like parents, and not through those who only superintend like the state, the more we see why the relation between the sexes must remain normally static and permanent.

Even when the education of the child has been completed and he grows into his own separate life, there develops in him a high sense of honor toward those who brought him into being. Everyone realizes how much he cost his parents in terms of care and sacrifice. Some, perhaps, never realize this completely until they themselves have children. But in varying degrees, all feel the need of "going back home" to pay loving tribute to a kind father and loving mother. The parents, too, in their old age look to their children, whom the mother nourished with her substance and the father with his labor, for a return of that affection bestowed on them during their youth. Thus, the sense of honor in children that makes them conscious of the debt of love to their parents, and the need of sympathy in parents that makes them crave the tribute of their children's affection, equally suggests that only a union that death alone can break can fully respond to the needs of the human heart.

*Marriage mirrors God's love for human nature*

Such is the natural reason for the permanence of marriage. In the supernatural order, the Church, after the manner of our blessed Lord, takes hold of this permanent character of love in the order of nature and elevates the promise "I do" to the dignity of a sacrament. The love that is always expressing itself in terms of the eternal, and articulating itself in such phrases as "till the sands of the desert grow cold," the Church seizes and refines by finding a symbol of love more abiding still than even the sands of the desert. She goes to the most personal, permanent, and unbreakable union of love the world has ever known — namely, the love of Christ for human nature — and during the solemnity of the nuptial Mass reminds the young couple that they are to love one another with the same indissoluble love with which our blessed Lord loved the human nature that He took from the womb of the Blessed Mother. That love which desires to express itself in terms of the permanent, the Church models on the great prototype of the marriage of God and man in the Incarnation of our Lord and Savior, Jesus Christ. When God veiled the awful terror of His glory, descended into the flesh-girt paradise of Mary, and assumed human nature,

He assumed it, not for an earthly life stretching from crib to Cross, but permanently and eternally through the risen life of Easter Sunday and the glorious Ascension to the right hand of the Father.

Now, since Christian marriage of flesh and flesh is modeled upon the permanent marriage of God and man, the Church says that it, too, must take on for life the character of permanence and indissolubility. As the womb of the Blessed Mother was the anvil of flesh upon which the divine and human natures of Christ were united under the Pentecostal flame of the Holy Spirit in the unity of the Person, so, too, the nuptial altar becomes the new anvil whereon two loving hearts are fused and joined by a flame of the sacramental Spirit in the unity of the flesh. Certainly this ideal of permanence is alone enough to transmute mere physical desire into something nobler than a Freudian urge, to elevate the permanence that natural love demands into an indissoluble bond that divine Love solicits, and to thrill young hearts to speak the words of Tobias: "For we are the children of saints, and we must not be joined together like heathens that know not God."[34]

Having reminded the young couple that their unity is modeled upon the inseparable union of God and man, the Church goes on to inquire what guarantees they will give that their love will be as permanent as their model, Jesus Christ. They may answer, "We will give our word." But the Church responds, "Nations have broken their word; human lovers have broken their vows before. Can you not give a better bond than this, that your love for one another will endure until death?" Then there comes from them the answer that the Church demands from every loving pair at her altar: "We will give the bond of our eternal salvation. We will seal it

---

[34] Tob. 8:5.

with our belief that the promise we make to one another is a promise made to God Himself, and if we are disloyal one to another, we shall forfeit the most precious thing in all the world — namely, our immortal souls."

When this bail of eternal salvation has been given, the Church seals it, not with a paper seal, but with the red seal of the precious Body and Blood of our Lord and Savior in the Communion of the Nuptial Mass. With their love thus bonded at the foot of the Cross, and the bail of their eternal salvation given in guarantee that in sickness and in health, in riches and poverty, they will love until death, the Church pronounces them man and wife.

As the priest sees them turn from the altar, united soul with soul and sealed with the blood of Christ, ere yet they are united body with body, he cannot help but think that such human love at such a peak is God on a pilgrimage to earth. They, too, realize as they go into their common life that it is not love which makes them marry, but consent. Love makes them want to marry, but it is their vow one to another, sealed with a seal of their eternal salvation, that makes them man and wife.

⚕

### The Church upholds the permanence of marriage

In the eyes of the Church, therefore, marriage is a permanent union patterned upon the abiding love of Christ for His Church, and not a terminable pact of selfish passion that endures only as long as the passion endures. By upholding such an ideal, by asking such a guarantee, and by teaching the sacredness of a vow, the Church makes marriage serious. She practically tells the young couple the same thing the sign over the cashier's desk tells the customer: "Count your change. No mistakes rectified after leaving the window."

71

No one in all the world loves lovers as much as the Church does — but only the lovers who mean what they say. Hence, the Church refuses to permit anyone to loosen the bond that has kept millions happy and stable, and therefore will not allow any man or woman, who gets himself or herself into a hole, to burrow like a mole and undermine the whole mountain of society. She believes that if people cannot mind their own business, which is the business of loyalty, then she will not free them to mind someone else's business, or someone else's babies. To her, the hilarity associated with divorce is like the hilarity of grave-diggers in a city swept by pestilence. She is opposed to divorce, not because she is unmodern, but because marriage makes people two in one flesh, and they can no more be severed during the incarnate life of their mutual love than a head can be severed from a body. She knows full well that if a man will not be a patriot in his own country, he will not be a patriot in another; and that if he will not continue to love the first woman whom he has chosen above all women in the world, then he must be suspected of telling the second the same vain promises. She asserts against the world that no rascal shall be regarded as respectful at that moment when he breaks from a loving wife and chooses another woman. She is willing to permit a woman to be released from a drunken husband, but she says that the woman must be content with that release, be satisfied with that experience, and not seek another while he lives. She believes in a release of this kind, but not when *release* is spelled with a hyphen.

There is a word that means little to nations that repudiate their bonds; there is a word that means nothing to men and women who repudiate their vows; but that same word means everything to those who unite themselves in a bond under our blessed Lord, who came to be the truth of the world, and that is the word *honor*. To those who still believe in it, each day brings, not the burden of a forced union, but the accord of heart and heart, and soul and soul. Just as two pieces of iron are fused into one by flame and fire, so, too, are the minds and hearts of husband and wife fused into one by the purging of mutual sacrifice and tribulation that brings them unto God. Succeeding years find them, not as two hearts with tangled and toneless strings, but an instrument so delicately attuned that love's skillful fingers need but brush over them to bring out their hidden beauties. The new vision of the flame of love comes to them, because they were faithful to its spark, and they see that:

> Not in marriage is the fulfillment of love, though its earthly and temporal fulfillment may be therein; for how can love, which is the desire of soul for soul, attain satisfaction in the conjunction of body with body? Poor indeed, if this were all the promise which love unfolded to us — the encountering light of two flames from within their close-shut lanterns. Therefore, sings Dante, and sing all noble poets after him, that love in this world is a pilgrim and a wanderer, journeying to the New Jerusalem; not here is the consummation of its yearnings, in that mere knocking at the gates of union which we christen marriage, but beyond the pillars of death and the corridors of the grave, in the union of spirit to spirit within the containing Spirit of God.[35]

[35] Francis Thompson.

Chapter Eight

❧

# Married couples
## must strive to
## live out the sacrament

⚛

Marriage is meant to be a bond breakable only by death, because love, by its nature, can be measured by neither space nor time. And yet, despite the ideal of marriage, the hard actualities of life make it end sometimes in dismal ruin and failure. A moment comes when the bonds once meant to be as firm as steel now seem as frail as a silken cord, and affection, which once was delicate, now begins to take things for granted.

It is at this stage that love needs a tonic, and loyalty needs re-enforcement. Something must be done to keep husband and wife together in order to fulfill their mutual social mission. The Church teaches that this tonic and re-enforcement is supplied by three things: first, by greater emphasis on love and less on mere sex; secondly, by loyalty to a vow; and thirdly, by love of children.

⚛
*Married couples must focus*
*on love, not on mere sex*

We are now living in what might be called the era of carnality. The Victorian pretended that sex did not exist; our age says that it is the only thing that exists. This one organic reaction has been so insanely magnified, boomed, popularized, vulgarized, and propagandized that it is no longer kept in its own place, like enjoying a meal, or laughing at a joke. Undoubtedly, sex has its particular part to play in life, but it is beautiful only when it is part of the whole — that is, part of that human nature given to us by Almighty God, which is not only biological, but also intellectual, moral, and religious. Its isolation from the whole nature of man and its consequent exaggeration has resulted in a wild orgy of frenzied filth, which has destroyed the sense of chivalry in men and the sense of delicacy in women. The Church has been dealing with marriage for twenty centuries, and yet nowhere in her marriage ceremony does she speak of sex, but she does speak of love. There is an important difference between the two.

Sex is like a lightning flash between two drifting clouds, a momentary brilliance followed by the dread rumblings of thunder. Love is less like a spark than a light, which goes out from the great white throne of God, permeating, infusing, and dwelling in hearts and attuning them to the vibrations of the great heart of God. Sex is a mutual conflict in which two hearts fall satiated and cry out at the goal, "Enough!" But love has no such word as *enough*, but only the word *always*.

Sex is a wild boar wallowing among the lilies and yet always thirsty, for those who break the lute in order to snare the music do so in vain. Love is as the flight of a bird suffering the loss of earth to purchase those higher and more rarefied levels where the spirit moves with the glorious liberty of the sons of God.

Hence, if any of the de-personalized and unsouled men and women of our day would recover the happiness of their married life, they must look *through* sex, to love, which reached its highest peak and its most sublime expression in the sacrifice of the Cross, where a God-man gave His life so that we might live it in abundance.

⚓

*Married couples must be mindful of their vow*

The second remedy for the tedium of marriage is loyalty to a vow, even from the psychological point of view. A marriage vow is the one thing that keeps couples together during the period of disillusionment and thus enables them to recover their happiness. It is a psychological fact that great pleasures are purchased only by surviving a moment of tedium, and great joys can be kept only on condition of enduring a moment of pain. It is only after the shock of the first cold plunge that we can enjoy the swim. It is only after long, weary hours of practice that we can enjoy rendering a sonata of Chopin. It is only after surviving the exercises of Latin grammar that we can enjoy the wisdom of Thomas Aquinas.[36] It is only after the exhaustion of the first mile's walk that we get our second wind and enjoy the thrill of exercise.

In like manner, it is only after the disillusionment that follows the first quarrel, or the irritation of the first extended visit of an unwelcome relative, that the couple get their second wind and begin to enjoy their union and their togetherness. It is only after the pain of the novitiate of self-wounding falls, which seem to be the dark night of the soul, that they discover the joy in lifting up one another to God. It is only after the tedium of killing their individual selfishness in mutual concession that they come to the pleasure of communion with one another. It is only from the ashes of self-love that they, Phoenix-like, rise to that permanent pleasure of mutual love which we call Christian marriage.

Having survived the Good Friday of disillusionment, thanks to their loyalty to a vow, the couple enter into the Easter of peace and

---

[36] St. Thomas Aquinas (c. 1225-1274), Dominican philosopher, theologian, and Doctor.

joy. The rivers of rapture deepen and broaden in the blended channel of love, and their mutual current flows on stronger, with the eddies of passion in the shallows. Then the insatiate rock and strain of physical emotion relaxes, and they begin to taste without fever the beautiful happiness of being together. Love, then, becomes more conscious of its Messiahship, busies itself more with the Father's business, and the couple's final reward for being faithful to the vow, for surviving the moment of monotony, is the pleasure of married life and the gift of a child from Heaven, which makes them an earthly trinity and proclaims that God has not yet despaired of men.

*Children bring new life to a marriage*

The third way to avoid the tedium of marriage is by making it fruitful. The love of husband for wife and wife for husband has its seasons of transports and ecstasies, but it also has its winter of disillusionment. The husband, after a few years of married life, makes a startling discovery that the wife is no longer a daughter of the gods, and the wife in her turn soon realizes that he is no longer her strong Apollo. The day soon comes when, under the magic but corroding touch of time, she loses the rose in her cheeks, which not even art can restore, and he forfeits the strong resolve to sacrifice all for his beloved, now even forgetting to send flowers on her birthday. Her childish prattle, which once made him laugh, now begins to get on his nerves, and his repetition of old wisecracks becomes as intolerable to her as his habit of spilling ashes on the carpet. Her mother, who once seemed sweet during the days of courtship, now overstays her visit, and his elder sister, who once seemed so jovial, is now a bore at the evening bridge table. She, who was once a joy to behold, is now commonplace, and he, who once was her pride, is now the routine companion of the breakfast table.

It is at this time, when beauty and strength have fled, that modern marriages founder and are broken on the rocks of misunderstanding. But it should not be so. Her beauty and his strength were not meant to be permanent possessions. Beauty and strength serve only the function of allurement. When beauty has allured, it passes away with pathetic dispatch; when strength has allured, it takes wings and flies. It is not in the nature of these things to continue.

But what can atone for their disappearance? What can save the couple from the prolonged tedium of their union?

At this time, when defects begin to appear, when others seem younger and fairer, stronger and sturdier, when love has lost its delicacy and the touch of the hand no longer thrills, there is nothing to counteract love's sad satiety, to crush mutual repulsion, to obliterate disillusionment, and to draw husband and wife out of themselves and make them rejoice in their mutual creation as a pair of baby arms which, encircling them with greater force than chains, makes them prisoners of love.

As the daughters are born, she begins to live again for him, and all her beauty is seen blooming once more in the second springtime of the little girls, who are nothing less than children of the gods. As the sons are born, he begins to live again for her, and all his strength and courage is seen flowering in the little boys, who are nothing less than young Apollos. All that was fair and then grew old is young again. All that was strong and then grew weak is strong again. Childish prattle no longer gets on his nerves, and although little Johnny would divest himself of the same wisecrack daily, she insists on having it repeated for each new visitor. Her mother now is not quite the crank he thought she was, as she nurses the sick baby, and his sister is not the bore she thought, as she supplies the playthings. The breakfast table now becomes peopled with happy faces, even though they sometimes do smile through tears and make human rainbows.

When Joan and Susanne make their First Communion, hands clasp that had almost forgotten to clasp. When Johnny serves his first Mass, lips meet that had not met since the scene over the visit of the mother-in-law. When Joe learns to say the Hail Mary, a new purpose of life possesses both: hopes for the future are reborn; the patter of little feet is like the song of birds announcing the springtime; affection becomes fresh; the allurements of beauty and strength return; and each new child who is born becomes another bead in the great rosary of love, uniting them in the imprisoning arms of God's little ones.

Eyes once bent earthward, after the manner of the beast that has missed its proper luminary, become, after the arrival of little children, eyes that look back to a home of long, long ago, in the little mountain town of Nazareth. There, under a flickering lamp, they see the strong and reverend stewardship of blessed Joseph, the selfless love of the sweetest of all mothers, Mary, and the loving, subject obedience of the Child who makes earth an outpost of Heaven.

There the father learns that true greatness depends, not on earthly success and garnered wealth, for Joseph, the guardian of Him to whom the earth and its fullness belonged, stood at a bench and handled the tools of a carpenter. The father's children learn lessons of obedience from the divine Child whom the winds and seas obeyed, and yet who was subject for thirty years to a village tradesman and a virgin. There the mother learns that men are prepared for great missions by noble women, and that, of all women, there is no model like the woman who was pure enough and beautiful enough to be the Mother of God, and from her, as the Mother of true Motherhood, there comes to parents these sweet reminders:

> *Your children are not your children.*
> *They are the sons and daughters of Life's longing*
>   *for itself.*
> *They come through you but not from you,*
> *And though they are with you, yet they belong*
>   *not to you.*
> *You may give them your love but not your thoughts,*
> *For they have their own thoughts.*
> *You may house their bodies but not their souls,*
> *For their souls dwell in the house of tomorrow,*
>   *which you cannot visit, not even in your dreams.*
>
> *You are the bows from which your children as living*
>   *arrows are sent forth.*
> *The Archer sees the mark upon the path of the infinite,*
>   *and He bends you with His might that His arrows*
>   *may go swift and far.*
> *Let your bending in the Archer's hand be for gladness;*
> *For even as He loves the arrow that flies, so He loves*
>   *also the bow that is stable.*[37]

---

[37] Reprinted from *The Prophet,* by Kahlil Gibran.

Chapter Nine

# Married couples
# help fill God's world

❧

Love seeks not only permanence, which accounts for the unbreakable bond of marriage, but also fruitfulness, which is the bearing of children. Married life should have a harvest, for all love should bear fruit. In order to understand the reasons for the fruitfulness of marriage, one must understand the meaning of love.

Love may be defined as mutual self-giving and self-outpouring, because love implies two persons who give themselves to one another. This is merely another way of saying that all love is sacrifice. Hence, the greatest joy in love is to throw oneself on the altar of the one loved. Its sweet feast is its own hunger and the wine of its own tears. Its richest banquet is to gird its loins and to serve. Its greatest jealousy is to be outdone by its cherished rival of the least advantage in self-giving, for without some spice of martyrdom, love's tastes are tasteless, and without the arrow that wounds, its quivers are barren and vain.

Because love is a mutual self-emptying, husband and wife vie with one another in the sacrifice of self. The woman sacrifices the irreparable that God has given her, that which makes her a virgin, that, too, which possibly is the hidden reason for her power to love but only once. The man, in his turn, sacrifices the liberty and freedom of his youth, the power to devote himself entirely to that love which he finds at the beginning of the journey of life. These two cups, one filled with beauty and innocence, the other with devotion and courage, flow one into another, as two rivers that run their course to the great ocean of the absorbing Love which is God.

But love is not only mutual self-giving; if it were but this, there would be only surrender. Love is not only mutual self-outpouring; if it were but this, it would be barren as a desert and would fructify nothing.

That which is surrendered but can never be recovered is the source of the tearful agony of loss. If love were only dual selfishness, with perpetual change and barter, like commerce between two shipwrecked sailors on a desert isle, it would yield no profit to either, but only be the enkindling of a flame in which each would be consumed.

Hence, love, in addition to being a giving or an outpouring, must also be a recovery. The escape from mere mutuality, which is death, is in a reciprocity that vies to give all, but is ever defeated by receiving. In other words, love must increase and multiply; it must recover itself in a harvest; it must, like the love of earth and tree, be fruitful unto new love. Something must result from love, for all love seeks to externalize itself as a gift and thus reproduce itself. That is why all love tends toward an incarnation. The husband and wife must have some reward and recovery for this sacrifice.

But how can their mutual self-outpouring end in self-recovery except by their two hearts conspiring against their individual impotence by filling up each at the store of the other their lacking measures, and thus building up, not the mere sum of themselves, but that new life which is a child and which gives to the winter of their marriage the springtime of fruit.

*The family reflects the Trinity*

Of what great love is this a reflection? Where is the model of the love that is mutual self-outpouring which ends in self-recovery? In this, as in all things, the Church finds the prototype of such a definition of love in that which is perfect Love — namely, God. The young couples who come to our altars for the nuptial Mass are told this, for in the solemn moment of that ceremony, their marriage is blessed in the name of the Trinity — Father, Son, and Holy Spirit — by which blessing their young hearts are lifted up beyond the straggling rays of love in their own hearts to Heaven itself, and the great fire of the triune love of God.

There is the prototype of all earthly love. In that never-ebbing tide of love, there is first of all mutual self-giving, in which the Father eternally begets a Son, who is His splendor, the glory of His substance, and the image of His infinite majesty. And the Son gives His whole self to the Father by praise and love in a Word that is divine.

But the love of Father for Son, and Son for Father, is not mere barren self-giving, for if it were only this, it would end in exhaustion. The Father loves the Son, and the Son loves the Father, and that mutual love for each other is so intense, so spiritual, so unworldly, so above earthly words, canticles, and embraces, that it can express itself only by that which signifies the fullness of love, and the recovery of self-giving — namely, a sigh! That is why that personal love of Father for Son is called the Holy Spirit, the Spirit of Love, in which the mutual outpouring of Father and Son recovers itself in the Holy Spirit, thus perfecting the cycle of the Godhead in an act of bliss unending.

There is the source of the definition of love as mutual self-outpouring which ends in self-recovery! There is the inspiration of married love that seeks, not only to exchange love for love, but also to reap interest in that exchange and to gather the harvest of a new life wherever the seed of a new life is sown. There in the very heart of the loving Trinity Itself is heard the call to every husband and wife to make of themselves an earthly trinity by recovering their mutual love in the bond of children.

⁂

*Married couples should welcome children*

Herein, too, is to be found the reason why the Church must always be opposed to any artificial attempts to restrict, limit, or prevent the fruit of love, even though they are heralded in the name of modern science and modern religion. The Church knows full well that such science is not real science, but only that poor travesty which knows enough to fumble forbidden levers with its baby fingers. Such religion is not real religion, but only an imitation whose power for mischief is out of all proportion to its love of God.

As war is not for the sport and loot of the private soldiers, and a plaything for their own selfish ambitions, so the gift of love is not for the pleasures of the organism. Husband and wife are sent out like the disciples of old, two by two, not to sit down to eat and drink, but to be fruitful apostles of love and to strive by their mutual loves to reinforce the ranks of life and love. Love has been given to them as a loan of divine Life, and it must be paid back into the bank of Life with life, and not with death. The divine fire of passion that fused man and woman was not given to scorch the flesh but to solder life, for "lust without life shall die," but "life without lust shall live."

To rob love of its fruit is to end love and ruin marriage. Just as the earth, which receives into its womb the grain that is destined to clothe it with golden harvest, must not be recreant to its gift of fostering life and kill the seed in its traitor-heart, so neither shall the love of husband and wife play traitor to all nature and all love by burying the talent of their fruitfulness in the napkin of their own voluntary barren selfishness.

Shall we not say in justice, then, that the man and woman who take the gift of love into their hearts, and then turn it against producing life, for the selfishness of their own pleasure, are betraying life and Love's great trust, stealing Heaven's fire, and enkindling the flame that consumes them and leaves naught but their dust behind?

Why, even if such a couple did not believe in God, even if they believed only in love, their own hearts of hearts should tell them that love was meant to be recovered in life, and that to be unfaithful to that gift of love and refuse to increase life, is to live in a world in which artists are always picking up brushes, but never finishing a picture; always lifting chisels, but never producing a statue; always touching bow to string, but never emitting a harmony; always having the springtime, but never the harvest. But this means putting an end to springtime for want of a harvest, filling the world with cages without birds, hives without bees, homes without children. It means filling the world with barren fig trees, which draw upon themselves the terrible curse of God.

To such men and women who spend their lives and leave nothing behind, who die little by little without passing on the torch of life, there must sometimes come the whisperings of a conscience that says:

> *Your cruelest pain is when you think of all*
> *The hoarded treasures of your body spent,*
> *And no new life to show. . . . Sometimes*
> *When darkness, silence and the sleeping world*

*Give vision scope, you lie awake and see*
*The pale, sad faces of the little ones*
*Who should have been your children, as they press*
*Their cheeks against your windows, looking in*
*With piteous wonder, homeless, famished babes,*
*Denied your wombs and bosoms.*[38]

*God shares with us the power of generating children*

How different is the conscience of those who obey the laws of love, which are the laws of God, and who therefore in their mutual self-giving recover their better selves in the youth and beauty of their offspring. How much the happiness of their lives belies those who say that in bringing children into the world, a woman imitates the beasts of the field. No! Rather does she imitate the very God who made her! Fecundity is of the spirit, more than of the flesh. Generation is not a push from below, but a gift from above. Generation belonged to God eternities before it was given to the flesh: "Shall not I, who make others bring forth children, myself bring forth, saith the Lord: Shall I that give generation to others myself be barren?"

From all eternity, God the Father generated a Son, the image of His glory, and from that day without beginning or end, the heavenly Father, in the ecstasy of the first and real paternity, has said to His Son, "Thou art My Son; this day have I begotten Thee."[39] This power of generating, God has communicated to mothers in order that they might prolong in time the power of God in eternity. The divine life by which God the Father draws from His eternal

[38] John Davidson.
[39] Ps. 2:7.

bosom, in the agelessness of eternity, a Son in His own image and likeness, God Himself communicates to mothers so that they may bring forth, in the flux and flow of time, His other children, or adopted sons who would be privileged to cry up to Him the sweetest of all prayers: "Our Father who art in Heaven."

⚘

### Mary is a model for all mothers

It is, therefore, a noble vocation to be a mother and, lest mothers lose sight of that great calling, they are bidden to look back upon that incomparable woman, Mary, who brought forth in Bethlehem the Eternal Word, our Lord and Savior, Jesus Christ. In her and by her, all women have received the mission to elevate, purify, and console man, and add their increment to the eternal harvest of souls. As she brought forth the cornerstone of the great spiritual edifice that is the Church, so every mother under her inspiration is to bring forth those living, eligible stones hewed from the great quarry of humanity to be shaped and cut by discipline and self-restraint to fit the great Cornerstone, which is Christ. As Mary brought forth from the virginal womb of her flesh the great Captain of salvation, so every Christian mother is to bring forth, not only from the womb of her flesh, but from the womb of the baptismal font, valiant soldiers of that great King and Captain, Christ. Under the sweet guardianship of that most beautiful of all mothers, every earthly mother is called, like her, to rock another cradle of the Holy Child, to bring forth a child destined to be a ruler of Israel, a Child of Mary, a Brother of Christ, a Son of the heavenly Father, and an heir of heaven — and what is Heaven but a nursery reserved only for children?

Every mother, under the vocation of God and the inspiration of the Blessed Mother, therefore, has a vision of Heaven, and there sees that whenever God gives to her a child, He forges for it, on the eternal anvil of Heaven, a golden crown of everlasting peace and joy. Her purpose and mission in life is to rear the child as a potential nobleman of the kingdom of God and then to give him back again to the heavenly Father, whence he came, in order that he might recover the crown that God made for him. For, after all, what is love but a mutual self-giving which ends in self-recovery, and what recovery is there in all time and space that is comparable to the recovery which is the discovery of God?

Chapter Ten

෴

# The loss of the sense of sin
# endangers God's world

∝

The gravest danger facing modern society, one that has brought the ruin of older civilizations and is destined to effect the collapse of our own, unless we prevent it, is the loss of the sense of sin. Remorse is almost an unknown passion, and penitent shame is but rarely felt. The burden of guilt does not rest on even a criminal's heart, and even good men look on deeds of infamy and acts of gross injustice and are not shocked. This is not because they are innocent, but because no sense of sin possesses their souls. There is a general denial that anything is wrong or that anything is right, and a general affirmation that what the older theological generation called sin is only a psychic evil or a fall in the evolutionary process.

Two principles inspire much of the personal and social dealings of many a citizen in our land: "What can I get out of it?" and "Can I get away with it?" Evil is confused with good, and good is confused with evil. Revolting books against virtue are termed "courageous"; those against morality are advertised as "daring and forward-looking"; and those against God are called "progressive and epoch-making." It has always been the characteristic of a generation in decay to paint the gates of Hell with the gold of Paradise. In a word, much of the so-called wisdom of our day is made up of that which once nailed our blessed Lord to the Cross.

It would be good for our generation to remember that the fires of Sinai still burn in the history of men and nations, that its dread thunders still roll across the centuries, and that the Cross which once was raised in defiance of sin will not be taken down until sin is vanquished and the Cross itself become the badge of eternal glory and triumph.

And in order that our day may know that sin is not just an arbitrary tag tacked on to human actions by the Church, or that it is not a mere fall in the evolutionary process, it might be profitable to inquire into the nature of sin by asking what nature thinks of sin, what conscience thinks of sin, and what God thinks of sin. Nature tells us that sin is death; conscience tells us that sin is guilt; and God tells us that sin is an offense against His divine love.

⚯

### *Sin is death*

Nature says that sin is death, a definition that Sacred Scripture confirms: "The wages of sin is death."[40] Death in the natural order is the domination of a lower order over a higher order, for the universe is made up of various levels or hierarchies, one subordinated to the other, such as the chemical, the vegetative, the animal, the human, and the divine.

If, for example, a rose is placed in a room filled with poisonous gas, it will die just as soon as the lower order, namely, the chemical, gains mastery over the higher order, which is that of life. The human body often dies through a slow wearing away and oxidation of its organism. At that precise point where there is a balance of forces in favor of the chemical process of oxidation as against the vital process, death ensues.

[40] Rom. 6:23.

Now, man has not only a body, but also a soul. As the life of the body is the soul, so the life of the soul is God. When, therefore, the body dominates the soul, the laws of the world dominate the laws of Christ, the flesh dominates the spirit, and the things of time dominate the things of eternity, there is a domination of a lower order over a higher order, and that domination or death we call sin. Sin, then, is a death in the strict sense of the term — namely the death of the life of God in the soul. In this sense, it is the Crucifixion all over again, for as often as we sin, we crucify Christ again in our hearts. Every soul is therefore a potential Calvary and every sin an actual cross:

> I saw the Son of God go by
> Crowned with a crown of thorns.
> "Was it not finished, Lord," said I,
> "And all the anguish borne?"
> He turned on me His awful eyes,
> "Hast thou not understood?
> Lo, every soul is a Calvary
> And every sin a rood."[41]

### Sin is guilt

Nature tells us that sin is death, but conscience tells us that it is guilt and that, as such, it is totally different from anything in the animal order and therefore something that is not a mere episode in the passage of nature and a thing that can be left behind, dead and done for. Nothing is more typical of the sense of human guilt than its power of asserting itself with unbated poignancy in spite

---

[41] Rachel A. Taylor.

of the lapse of time. Society may forgive the transgressor, but the transgressor does not forgive himself. His friends may cease to blame him, but he does not cease to blame himself. Others may forget it, but he does not forget. He knows he cannot forgive himself, but that he must be forgiven; and his horror-crammed memory cries out:

> Canst thou not minister to a mind diseased,
> Pluck from the memory a rooted sorrow,
> Raze out the written troubles of the brain,
> And with some sweet oblivious antidote
> Cleanse the stuff'd bosom of that perilous stuff
> Which weighs upon the heart?

How can we explain this sense of guilt and this indelible remorse except in reference to a Person who has claims of love upon us? How explain this pain of the soul except as a deordination against the God of justice and love? If a magnetic needle were endowed with feeling and it pointed south instead of north, it would be in pain, because it would not be pointing in the direction of its true nature. If a bone becomes dislocated, the whole body suffers, because the bone is not where it ought to be. In like manner, if the heart and mind and soul of man, by a free act of choice, turn not to the God of love and mercy, but away from Him to the things of self, he, too, suffers pain and remorse, because he is not where he ought to be — in the arms of God.

Since past guilt endures in us as living past, and not as a dead past, like the facts of history, it must be something over which we have the power to make or unmake. The real reason why the guilt endures is not that it may crush us beneath its weight, but that we might carry it up the hill of Calvary to the foot of the Cross, there to ask the loving Savior to detach His arm from the Cross and lift it over our souls in forgiving pardon and absolution. And so it is that from Genesis to the book of Revelation there is heard, like the wail of the wind and the sob of the sea, a cry on the air of stricken humanity, confessing to its God, whose property is always to have mercy and to spare: "I have sinned before my Father who is in Heaven."

❧

### Sin is an offense against God's love

And that brings us to what God thinks of sin. In a great city of the East — famous for its history and splendors — it is evening. Sleep has come to the eyes of men, except for a small group of the wicked, which, with a white-faced traitor in its midst, is plotting against the Innocent. Outside the city runs a brook called the Kedron, and beyond, on a sloping hill, is a wood of small, stunted, bushy trees, known as the Garden of Gethsemane.

The figures of four men cross this brook, and without a word, they sink into the enveloping darkness.

Just as soon as the familiar olive trees present themselves to their gaze, One of the four sees what the other three cannot see. That One, our blessed Lord, sees there in the dark garden, the mighty array, the tremendous array, of all the sins that ever were committed or that would be committed down to the end of time, for His Father in Heaven was about to lay upon Him the iniquities of us all. No wonder, then, that He turns to His companions, saying, "Stay you here and watch with me. My soul is sorrowful, even unto death."[42]

Leaving them, He enters the gloomy place, summoning all the courage of God, all the infinite resources of His love, the great

---

[42] Cf. Matt. 26:38.

thought that if He were about to be destroyed, humanity was about to be saved. Fearlessly He moves into the depths of Gethsemane. About as far from His companions as a man could throw a stone, in the murky recesses of that forest, He throws Himself upon the ground and prays: "O Father, if it be possible, let this chalice pass from me," but immediately He adds, "Yet, not my will but Thine be done."[43]

Turning, for the Father's will is indicated to Him in a voice from Heaven, He bares His innocent breast, He puts out His sinless hands, and He allows an ocean wave of sin to flow in upon Him and overwhelm Him. Then that mighty Soul lifts up His hands, as if with more than Samson's strength He were to pull down the heavens upon Him, draws down the storm of God's eternal justice and lies crushed beneath it — a plaintive, human life, almost extinguished, but not extinguished, because it was divine life as well as human. The fountains of His heart are moved, and, drop by drop, through the burning pores of His skin, beads of blood fall to the ground as a red rosary of redemption — and one single drop would have been enough to have redeemed ten thousand worlds!

From the north and the south, from the east and the west, the gathering storm of sin rolls up, discharging itself as a torrent upon our blessed Lord. "Hopes blighted, vows broken, opportunities lost, innocence betrayed, penitence relapsing, the aged failing; the sophistry of misbelief, the willfulness of doubt, the tyranny of passion, the canker of remorse, the wasting force of care, the anguish of shame, the agony of disappointment, the sickness of despair. . . ."[44]

---

[43] Cf. Matt. 26:39; Luke 22:42.

[44] Cf. John Henry Newman, Discourse 16: "Mental Sufferings of Our Lord in His Passion."

Never was a curse or imprecation uttered, never was a word impure or venomous spoken, never was a blasphemous oath hurled against Heaven that does not seem to stain His lips, for the sins of the world are upon Him. Never was there an open act of evil or a secret deed of shame that does not seem to be thrust into His hands, so that He, as if the guilty one, might bear its load of corruption, for the sins of the world are upon Him. Never was there an inmost thought of evil, a cherished foul desire, that does not attempt to creep into His mind and heart, as though its sin and corruption, too, were His, for the sins of the world are upon Him.

The first sin of Adam and Eve down to the last sin that will be committed at the crack of doom is heaped upon Him. Cain is there, purple in the sheet of his brother's blood. There, too, were the sins of the sons and daughters of Israel rotting the earth with the leprosy of their revolt; the lusts and wickedness of men before the flood; the impurities of Sodom and Gomorrah; and the pagan idolatries of the pagan hordes who gathered around the altars of false gods.

The world of the future is there with its sins — sins that rent Christ's Mystical Body — sins of brutish vice; sins of Christian people, whose crimes taught deeper baseness to the heathen and lower coarseness to the pagan; sins deadly in their malice, hideous in their nature; sins that make the heart of Christ sick with sorrow; sins too loathsome to be mentioned; sins too terrible to be named; sins committed in the glare of the noonday sun under the very eyes of God; sins committed in the darkness of night, through which it was hoped the eyes of God could not pierce; sins committed in the country, which made nature shudder; sins committed in the city, in the city's atmosphere of sin; sins of the old, who should have passed the age of sinning; sins of the young, for whom the heart of Christ is tenderly pierced; sins that destroyed Paradise; sins that

ruined the earth; sins that shut the gates of Heaven; sins that
broke down the law; sins that trampled love; sins that had brought
men to Hell; sins that now brought God to earth; sins of those who
say there is no God; sins of war; sins of peace; sins of those who say
there is no sin!

Chapter Eleven

# God will judge every person by how he lives

❧

There comes a time in the life of every man when at the supreme and tragic hour of death, his friends and relatives ask, "How much did he leave?" It is just at that split second God is asking, "How much did he take with him?" It is only the latter question that matters, for it is only our works that follow us.

The story of life is brief: "It is appointed unto men once to die and after this the judgment," for "the Son of Man shall come in the glory of His Father with His angels, and then will He render to every man according to his works."[45] In the general forgetfulness of the Christian religion, which has passed over our civilization like a foul miasma, this great truth that a judgment follows death has been ignored in the moral outlook of the universe. Our souls can profit much from meditation upon it and its two important features: its necessity and its nature.

❧

*Judgment is necessary*

All nature testifies to the necessity of judgment. Everywhere below man, nature reveals itself as passing sentence on those who

[45] Heb. 9:27; Matt. 16:27.

refuse to obey her laws. We need only look around us in the hospitals, prisons, and asylums to see that nature, like a judge seated in judgment, is squaring her accounts with those who violate her laws. If the body has abused itself by excess, nature takes revenge and passes the judgment of disease and infirmity. If a fragment of a star breaks from its central core and swings out of its orbit, nature passes the judgment that it shall burn itself out in space.

Nature settles her account with natural things here and now. But the moral side of the universe has not made its lasting reckoning with every man on this side of the grave: there is too much anguished innocence, too much unpunished wrong, too much suffering of the good, too much prosperity of the evil, too much pain for those who obey God's laws, too much pleasure for those who disobey them, too much good repute for those who sin unseen, too much scorn for those who pray unseen, too many unsung saints, too many glorified sinners, too many Pilates who act as righteous judges, too many Christs who go down to crucifixion, too many proud and vain souls who say, "I have sinned, and nothing has happened."

But the reckoning day must come, and just as once a year each businessman must balance his accounts, so, too, that important hour must come when every soul must balance its accounts before God. For life is like a cash register, in that every account, every thought, every deed, like every sale, is registered and recorded. And when the business of life is finally done, God pulls from out of the registry of our souls that slip of our memory on which is recorded our merits and demerits, our virtues and our vices — the basis of the judgment on which shall be decided eternal life or eternal death. We may falsify our accounts until that day of judgment, for God permits the wheat and the cockle to grow unto the harvest, but then, "in the time of the harvest, I will say to the reaper: Gather up first the cockle and bind it into bundles to burn, but the wheat gather ye into my barn."[46]

⚬

### Judgment is recognized by God and the soul

But what is the nature of judgment? In answer to this question, we are more concerned with the particular judgment at the moment of death, than with the general judgment, when all nations of the earth stand before their God. Judgment is recognition both on the part of God and on the part of the soul.

First of all, it is recognition on the part of God. Imagine two souls appearing before the sight of God, one in the state of grace, the other in the state of sin. Grace is a participation in the nature and life of God. Just as a man participates in the nature and life of his parents by being born of his parents, so, too, a man who is born of the Spirit of God by Baptism participates in the nature of God: the life of God, as it were, flows through his veins, imprinting an unseen but genuine likeness.

When, therefore, God looks upon a soul in the state of grace, He sees in it a likeness of His own nature. Just as a father recognizes his own son because of likeness of nature, so, too, Christ recognizes the soul in the state of grace in virtue of resemblance to Him and says to the soul: "Come, ye blessed of my Father: I am the natural Son, you are the adopted son. Come into the kingdom prepared for you from all eternity."[47]

God looks into the other soul that is in the state of sin and has not that likeness, and just as a father knows his neighbor's son is not his own, so, too, God looking at the sinful soul and, failing to

[46] Matt. 13:30.
[47] Cf. Matt. 25:34.

see therein the likeness of His own flesh and blood, does not recognize it as His own kind, and says to it, as He said in the parable of the bridegroom, "I know you not."[48] And it is a terrible thing not to be known by God.

Not only is sin a recognition from God's point of view, but it is also a recognition from man's point of view. Just suppose that while cleaning your car, or your house, a very distinguished person was announced at the door. You would probably act differently than if you were thoroughly clean, well dressed, and presentable. In such an unclean condition, you would ask to be excused, saying you were not fit to appear in the sight of such a person.

When a soul is before the sight of God, it acts in much the same manner. Standing before the tremendous majestic presence of Almighty God, it does not plead, it does not argue, it does not entreat, it does not demand a second hearing. It does not protest the judgment, for it sees itself as it really is. In a certain sense, it judges itself, God merely sealing the judgment.

If it sees itself clean and alive with the life of God, it runs to the embrace of Love, which is Heaven, just as a bird released from its cage soars into the skies. If it sees itself slightly stained and the robes of its baptism remediably soiled, it protests that it is not to enter into the sight of Purity, and hence throws itself into the purifying flames of Purgatory. If it sees itself irremediably vitiated, having no likeness whatever to the purity and holiness of God, if it has lost all affection for the things of spirit, then it could no more endure the presence of God than a man who abhors beauty could endure the pleasure of music, art, and poetry. Why, Heaven would be Hell to such a soul, for it would be as much out of place in the holiness of Heaven as a fish out of water. Hence, recognizing its own

---

[48] Matt. 25:12.

unworthiness, its own unholiness, its own ungodliness, its own distaste for the purity of God, it casts itself into Hell in the same way that a stone, released from the hand, falls to the ground.

Only three states, therefore, are possible after the particular judgment: Heaven, Purgatory, and Hell. Heaven is love without pain; Purgatory is pain with love; Hell is pain without love.

⚘

### Each soul will face judgment

Such is judgment! And oh, how much better the present age would be if it lived in the habitual temper of men who remembered that they had an account to give! How much more justice would reign in our economic and social life if all men walked in fear of the judgment that is to come! How much happier life would be if each realized that there are only two beings in all the world: our soul and the God who made it. Our emphasis on the group and on the nation and on the masses has made us oblivious to the great truth lying behind the judgment: that we are all individual souls responsible to God. We find ourselves talking of society as if it were a permanent thing, forgetting that it is really the passing of separate immortal persons into an unseen state, that while some slip away and others steal in, the flux and influx is the going of individual personal existences, each of which is worthy of redemption. We talk of masses of human beings as of a counter that was cleared from time to time, all the while forgetting the pathetic truth that all is not over with those whom history describes.

I wonder if a general ever thinks of the value of each soul and the responsibility it has to give when he sends his army into a storm of steel and shell. I wonder if the university professor realizes it, as he poisons the souls of his students with his sophistry and leaves not a hope behind. I wonder if we, as we walk the streets, jostle the crowds, hustle into subways, mingle with mobs, and push into theaters are fully conscious that the men and women who make up these groups are endowed with immortal souls and are responsible for each and every conscious act, down even to the last.

I wonder if we remember that all that is past and done in human history has one day to be revived into living and eternal interest at the judgment seat of God. All those men and women of history who figure in the scrolls of time, whose reality seems more like the characters of a story, whose names we cover with praise or insult, whose deeds we loath or imitate — all those peacemakers and mischief-makers, saints and sinners, saviors and betrayers of nations, lords and peasants; all the Egyptians who mused before the silence of their sphinx and paid tribute to their dead before the stony jute of the pyramids; all the great ones of the earth whose names are carved in granite and all the poor ones whose names are painted on wood; the thief at the right hand and the thief at the left hand; Mary Magdalene and the Pharisees; Nero and Paul, Alexander, Caesar, Bismarck, Napoleon, Washington, Lincoln: all these lived, and they had their likings and their hates, their loves and their hopes. They gained what they thought was worthwhile, and enjoyed what they thought was best, and what each one did in his flesh is determining his present destiny. The door of their opportunities is shut, and they have rendered an account of their stewardship, and like them, each one of us individually is reserved for a day when we shall be judged, not by public opinion, but by the eternal Christ coming with His Cross in the clouds of Heaven to render to every man according to his works.

We can, therefore, be sure of nothing while eternity is in doubt, but while there is life, there is hope, there is opportunity! While our days are with us, there is Heaven and happiness within our reach if we be faithful, virtuous, and simple of heart, and make friends with the Judge. The longest day has its evening, and after the evening comes the darkness of night. Christ crucified has no redemptive relation with the dead: He has either redeemed them, or they are beyond the reach of redemption. While we yet have life, the pierced hands of Christ are outstretched to beckon us onward to drink the wine of love from the great chalice of His Sacred Heart. But when our soul has passed the gate of eternity, those pierced hands, which all during life we saw outstretched on the Cross, will detach themselves and fold together in judgment. May we be caught within the folded embrace as eternally captured captives of His redemptive love!

Chapter Twelve

⚘

# God purifies
# souls after death

⁂

There is one word that to modern ears probably signifies the unreal, the fictional, and even the absurd in the Christian vision of life, and that is the word *Purgatory*. Although the Christian world believed in it for sixteen centuries, for the last three hundred years it has ceased to be a belief outside the Church and has been regarded as a mere product of the imagination, rather than as a fruit of sound reason and inspiration.

It is quite true to say that the belief in Purgatory has declined in just the proportion that the modern mind forgot the two most important things in the world: the purity of God and the heinousness of sin. Once both of these vital beliefs are admitted, the doctrine of Purgatory is inescapable.

For what is Purgatory but a place or condition of temporal punishment for those who depart this life in God's grace, but are not entirely free from venial faults or have not entirely paid the satisfaction due to their transgression? In simpler language, love without suffering is Heaven; suffering without love is Hell; and suffering with love is Purgatory.

Purgatory is that place in which the love of God tempers the justice of God, and secondly, where the love of man tempers the injustice of man.

✿

*God's mercy and justice necessitate Purgatory's existence*

First, Purgatory is where the love of God tempers the justice of God. The necessity of Purgatory is grounded upon the absolute purity of God. In the book of Revelation we read of the great beauty of His city, of the pure gold, with its walls of jasper and its spotless light, which is not of the sun or moon but the light of the Lamb slain from the beginning of the world. We also learn of the condition of entering the gates of that heavenly Jerusalem: "There shall not enter into it anything defiled, or that worketh abomination, or maketh a lie, but they that are written in the book of the life of the Lamb."[49]

Justice demands that nothing unclean, but only the pure of heart shall stand before the face of a pure God. If there were no Purgatory, then the justice of God would be too terrible for words, for who are they who would dare assert themselves pure enough and spotless enough to stand before the immaculate Lamb of God? The martyrs who sprinkled the sands of the Coliseum with their blood in testimony of their Faith? Most certainly! The missionaries like Paul who spend themselves and are spent for the spread of the Gospel? Most assuredly! The cloistered saints who in the quiet calm of a voluntary Calvary become martyrs without recognition? Most truly! But these are glorious exceptions. How many millions there are who die with their souls stained with venial sin, who have known evil, and by their strong resolve have drawn from it only to carry with them the weakness of their past as a leaden weight.

The day we were baptized, the Church laid upon us a white garment with the injunction: "Receive this white garment, which

---

[49] Rev. 21:27.

mayest thou carry without stain before the judgment seat of our Lord Jesus Christ, that thou mayest have life everlasting." How many of us during life have kept that garment unspotted and un-soiled by sin so that we might enter immediately upon death into the white-robed army of the King? How many souls departing this life have the courage to say that they left it without any undue at-tachment to creatures and that they were never guilty of a wasted talent, a slight cupidity, an uncharitable deed, a neglect of holy in-spiration, or even an idle word, for which every one of us must ren-der an account? How many souls there are gathered in at the deathbed, like late-season flowers, that are absolved from sins, but not from the debt of their sins?

Take any of our national heroes whose names we venerate and whose deeds we emulate. Would any Englishman or American who knew something of the purity of God, as much as he loves and re-spects the virtues of a Lord Nelson or a George Washington, really believe that either of them at death were free enough from slight faults to enter immediately into the presence of God? Why, the very nationalism of a Nelson or a Washington, which made them both heroes in war, might in a way make them suspect of being unsuited the second after death for that true internationalism of Heaven, where there is neither English nor American, Jew nor Greek, barbarian nor free, but all one in Christ Jesus, our Lord.

All these souls who die with some love of God possessing them are beautiful souls, but if there is no Purgatory, then because of their slight imperfections they must be rejected without pity by di-vine justice. Take away Purgatory, and God could not pardon so easily, for will an act of contrition at the edge of the tomb atone for thirty years of sinning? Take away Purgatory, and the infinite jus-tice of God would have to reject from Heaven those who resolve to pay their debts, but have not yet paid the last farthing.

Purgatory is where the love of God tempers the justice of God, for there God pardons because He has time to retouch these souls with His Cross, to recut them with the chisel of suffering, that they might fit into the great spiritual edifice of the heavenly Jerusalem; to plunge them into that purifying place where they might wash their stained baptismal robes to be fit to enter into the spotless purity of Heaven; to resurrect them like the Phoenix of old from the ashes of their own sufferings, so that, like wounded eagles healed by the magic touch of God's cleansing flames, they might mount heavenward to the city of the pure, where Christ is King and Mary is Queen, for, regardless of how trivial the fault, God cannot pardon without tears, and there are no tears in Heaven.

⚬

*Purgatory enables us to atone*
*for our lack of love for others*

On the other hand, Purgatory is a place, not only where the love of God tempers the justice of God, but where the love of man may temper the injustice of man. Most men and women are quite unconscious of the injustice, the ingratitude, and the thanklessness of their lives until the cold hand of death is laid upon one whom they love. It is then, and only then, that they realize (and oh, with what regret!) the haunting poverty of their love and kindness. One of the reasons why the bitterest of tears are shed over graves is because of words left unsaid and deeds left undone. "The child never knew how much I loved her." "He never knew how much he meant to me." "I never knew how dear he was until he was gone." Such words are the poisoned arrows that cruel death shoots at our hearts from the door of every sepulcher.

Oh, then we realize how differently we would have acted if only the departed one could come back again. Tears are shed in vain before eyes that cannot see, caresses are offered without response to arms that cannot embrace, and sighs do not stir a heart whose ear is deaf. Oh, then the anguish for not offering the flowers before death had come and for not sprinkling the incense while the beloved was still alive and for not speaking the kind words that now must die on the very air they cleave. Oh, the sorrow at the thought that we cannot atone for the stinted affection we gave them, for the light answers we returned to their pleading, and for the lack of reverence we showed to one who was perhaps the dearest thing that God had ever given us to know. Alas, too late! It does little good to water last year's crop, to snare the bird that has flown, or to gather the rose that has withered and died.

Purgatory is a place where the love of God tempers the justice of God, but also where the love of man tempers the injustice of man, for it enables hearts who are left behind to break the barriers of time and death, to convert unspoken words into prayers, unburned incense into sacrifice, unoffered flowers into alms, and undone acts of kindness into help for eternal life.

Take away Purgatory, and how bitter would be our grief for our unkindnesses and how piercing our sorrow for our forgetfulness. Take away Purgatory, and how meaningless are our memorial and armistice days, when we venerate the memory of our dead. Take away Purgatory, and how empty are our wreaths, our bowed heads, our moments of silence.

But, if there is a Purgatory, then immediately the bowed head gives way to the bent knee, the moment of silence to a moment of prayer, and the fading wreath to the abiding offering of the sacrifice of that great Hero of heroes, Christ.

Purgatory, then, enables us to atone for our ingratitude because, through our prayers, mortifications, and sacrifices, it makes it possible to bring joy and consolation to the ones we love. Love is stronger than death, and hence, there should be love for those who have gone before us. We are the offspring of their life, the gathered fruit of their labor, the solicitude of their hearts. Shall death cut off our gratitude? Shall the grave stop our love? Shall the cold clod prevent the atoning of our ingratitude? The Church assures us that, not being able to give more to them in this world, since they are not of it, we can still seek them out in the hands of divine justice and give them the assurance of our love and the purchasing price of their redemption.

Just as the man who dies in debt has the maledictions of his creditors following him to the grave, but may have his good name respected and revered by the labor of his son who pays the last penny, so, too, the soul of a friend who has gone to death owing a debt of penance to God may have it remitted by us who are left behind, by minting the gold of daily actions in the spiritual coin which purchases redemption. Into the crucibles of God, these departed souls go like stained gold to have their dross burned away by the flames of love. These souls, who have not died in enmity with God, but have fallen wounded on the battlefield of life, fighting for the victory of His cause, have not the strength to bind their own wounds and heal their own scars. It remains for us who are still strong and healthy, clad with the armor of faith and the shield of salvation, to heal their wounds and make them whole that they might join the ranks of the victors and march in the procession of the conquerors. We may be sure that if the penny that gives bread to the hungry body delivers a soul to the table of our Lord, it will never forget us when it enters into the homeland of victory.

While yet confined to that prison of purifying fire, they hear the voices of the angels and saints who call them to their true fatherland, but they are incapable of breaking their chains, for their time of merit is passed. Certainly God cannot be unmindful of a wife who offers her merits to the captive soul of a husband waiting for his deliverance. Surely the mercy of God cannot be such that He would be deaf to the good works of a mother who offers them for the liberation of her offspring who are yet stained with the sins of the world. Surely God will not forbid such communication of the living with the dead, since the great act of Redemption is founded on the reversibility of merits.

Responsive, then, will we be to the plea, not only of our relatives and friends, but of that great mass of unarmed warriors of the Church Suffering who are yet wearing the ragged remnants of sin, but who, in their anxiety of soul to be clothed in the royal robes fit for entrance into the palace of the King, cry out to our responsive hearts the plaintive and tender plea: "Have mercy on me, have mercy on me, at least you, my friends, for the hand of the Lord has touched me."

Chapter Thirteen

# Hell is for those who willfully reject God

If there is any subject that is offensive to modern sentimentalists, it is the subject of Hell. Our generation clamors for what the poet has called "a soft dean . . . who never mentions hell to ears polite,"[50] and our unsouled age wants a Christianity watered so as to make the gospel of Christ nothing more than a gentle doctrine of good-will, a social program of economic betterment, and a mild scheme of progressive idealism.

There are many reasons why the modern world has ceased to believe in Hell, among which we may mention, first, a psychological reason. If a man has led a very wicked life, he does not want to be disturbed in his wrongdoings by harsh words about justice. His wish that there be no final punishment for his crimes thus becomes father to the thought that there is no such thing as Hell. That is why the wicked man denies Hell, whereas the saint never denies it, but only fears it.

Another reason for the denial of Hell is that some minds confuse the crude imagery of poets and painters with the reality of the moral order behind the doctrine. Eternal realities are not always easy to portray in the symbols of time and space, but that is no

---

[50] Alexander Pope, *Moral Essays*, Epistle 4, line 149.

reason why they should be denied by anyone, any more than the reality of America should be denied because it is sometimes symbolized by a woman bearing a flag of red, white, and blue.

A final reason is found in the reason that the doctrine of Hell has been isolated from the organic whole of Christian truths. Once it is separated from the doctrines of sin, freedom, virtue, redemption, and justice, it becomes as absurd as an eye separated from the body. The justice of this reasoning is borne out in the fact that men become scandalized about Hell when they cease to be scandalized about sin. The Church has never altered one single iota the belief in an eternal Hell as taught by her Founder, our Lord and Savior, Jesus Christ. In adherence to His divine testimony, the Church teaches, first, that Hell is a demand of justice, and secondly, that Hell is a demand of love.

⚬

### Justice demands Hell's existence

First, once it is recognized that the moral order is grounded on justice, then retribution beyond the grave becomes a necessity. All peoples have held it morally intolerable that by the mere fact of dying, a murderer or an impenitent wrongdoer should triumphantly escape justice. The same fate cannot lie in store for the martyr and the persecutor, Nero and Paul, the Judas and Christ. If there is a supreme good to which man can attain only by courageous effort, it must follow that the man who neglects to make that effort imperils his felicity. Once it is granted that eternal life is a thing that has to be won, there must always be the grim possibility that it may also be lost.

Even the order of nature itself suggests retribution for every violation of a law. There is a physical law to the effect that for every action, there is a contrary and equal reaction. If, for example, I stretch a rubber band three inches, it will react with a force equal to three inches. If I stretch it six inches, it will react with a force equal to six inches. If I stretch it twelve inches, it will react with a force equal to a foot. This physical law has its counterpart in the moral order, in which every sin necessarily implies punishment. What is sin but an action against a certain order?

There are three orders against which a man may sin: first, the order of individual conscience; secondly, the order of the union of consciences, or the state; and thirdly, the source of both, or God. Now, if I sin or act against my conscience, there is a necessary re-action in the form of remorse of conscience, which, in normal individuals, varies with the gravity of the sin committed.

Secondly, if I act or sin against the union of consciences, or the state, there is a contrary and equal reaction that takes the form of a fine, imprisonment, or death sentence meted out by the state. It is worthy of note that the punishment is never determined by the length of time required to commit the crime, but rather, by the nature of the crime itself. It takes only a second to commit murder, and yet the state will take away life for such an offense.

Finally, whenever I sin against God, and this I do when I rebel either against the order of conscience or state, I am acting contrary to One who is infinite. For this action, there is bound to be a reaction. The reaction from the Infinite must, therefore, be infinite, and an infinite reaction from God is an infinite separation from God. And an infinite separation from God is an eternal divorce from life and truth and love, and an eternal divorce from life and truth and love is Hell!

It should be evident, therefore, that eternal punishment is not an arbitrary construction of theologians, but is the very counterpart of sin. We are too often wont to look upon Hell as an afterthought in the mind of God and regard it as related to sin in the same way that a spanking is related to an act of disobedience on the part of a child. This is not true. The punishment of spanking is something that does not necessarily follow upon an act of disobedience. It may be a consequence, but it need not be. Rather, it is true to say that Hell is related to a sinful and evil life in the same way that blindness is related to the plucking out of an eye, for the two are inseparable. One necessarily follows the other. Life is a harvest, and we reap what we sow: if we sow in sin, we reap corruption; but if we sow in the spirit, we reap life everlasting.

The teaching of our Lord bears out this demand of justice, for His doctrine was not merely an amiable gospel of indifference, as His own life was not one of sentimental good-naturedness. He very distinctly taught that men might do things that would prove their undoing. Never did He give assurance that He would succeed with everyone. The very fact that He poured out His life's blood to redeem us from sin could only mean that sin might have such a terrible consequence as Hell. For, on the last day, the good shall be separated from the bad, and the sheep from the goats:

Then shall the King say to them that shall be on His right hand: "Come, ye blessed of my Father, possess you the kingdom prepared for you from the foundation of the world. For I was hungry, and you gave me to eat; I was thirsty, and you gave me drink; I was a stranger, and you took me in. . . . Amen, I say to you, as long as you did it to one of these my least brethren, you did it to me." Then He shall say to them also that shall be on His left hand: "Depart from me, you cursed, into everlasting fire which was prepared for the Devil and his angels. For I was hungry, and you gave me not to eat: I was thirsty, and you gave me not to drink. I was a stranger, and you took me not in. . . . As long as you did it not to one of these least, neither did you do it to me." And these shall go into everlasting punishment, but the just, into life everlasting.[51]

These are the words of the Son of God, who is Truth itself, and it is difficult to understand why anyone, knowing and admitting this, would accept His words concerning Heaven and deny His words concerning Hell. If He is worthy of belief in one instance, He must be worthy of belief in another.

⚘

### Love itself necessitates Hell's existence

Hell is demanded, not only by justice, but also by love. The failure to look upon Hell as involving love makes men ask the question "How can a God of love create a place of everlasting punishment?" This is like asking why a God of love should be a God of justice. It forgets that the sun, which warms so gently, may also cause something to wither, and the rain, which nourishes so tenderly, may also cause something to rot.

Those who cannot reconcile the God of love with Hell do not know the meaning of love. There is nothing sweeter than love; there is nothing more bitter than love; there is nothing that so much unites souls and so much separates them as love. Love demands reciprocity; love seeks a lover; and when love finds reciprocity, there is a fusion and a compenetration and a union to a sublime and ecstatic degree. And when it is a question of the love of God and the love of the soul, that is the happiness of Heaven.

But suppose that love does not find reciprocity; or suppose that love does find it, only to be betrayed, spurned, and rejected. Can

[51] Matt. 25:34-46.

love still forgive? Love can forgive injuries and betrayals and insults, and divine love can forgive even to seventy times seven. But there is only one thing in the world that human love cannot forgive, and there is only one thing in eternity that divine love cannot forgive, and that is the refusal to love. When, therefore, the soul by a final free act refuses to return human love for divine love, then divine love abandons it to its own selfishness, to its own solitariness, to its own loneliness. And what punishment in all the world is comparable to being abandoned, not by the lovely but by the Love which is God?

Love forgives everything except one thing, and that is the refusal to love. A human heart pursues another and appeals for its affection with all the purity and high ardor of its being. It showers the loved one with gifts, tokens of sacrifice, and all the while remains most worthy of a responding affection. But if, after a long and weary pursuit, it has only been spurned and rejected and betrayed, that human heart turns away and bursting with a pent-up emotion in obedience to the law of love, cries out, "Love has done all that it can. I can forgive anything except the refusal to love."

Something of this kind takes place in the spiritual order. God is the Great Lover on the quest of His spouse, which is the human soul. He showers it with gifts, admits it into His royal family in the sacrament of Baptism, into His royal army in the sacrament of Confirmation, and invites it to His royal table in the sacrament of the Everlasting Bread, and countless times during human life whispers to it in health and sickness, in sorrow and joy, to respond to His plaintive pleadings, abandon a life of sin, and return love for love. If, however, the human heart, after rejecting this love many times only to be loved again, after ignoring the knock of Christ at the door of his soul only to hear the knock again, finally, at the moment of death completely spurns and rejects that divine goodness, then the God of love, in obedience to the law of love, cries out, "Love has done all that it can. I can forgive everything, except the refusal to love."

And it is a terrible thing to be through with love, for once divine love departs at death, it never returns. That is why Hell is eternal! That is why Hell is a place where there is no love!

Chapter Fourteen

# How we find our place in God's world

⚜

One of the greatest tragedies of history is that He who carpentered the universe was carpentered to a Cross. There is tragic irony in the fact that He who spent most of His life in handling wood and nails and crossbeams met His end on a deathbed made of those very things. One of our own American priest-poets has described in touching language how the nails of the carpenter shop became the nails of the Carpenter's Cross.

> *Whenever the bright blue nails would drop*
> *Down on the floor of his carpenter shop,*
> *St. Joseph, prince of carpenter men,*
> *Would stoop to gather them up again;*
> *For he feared for two little sandals sweet;*
> *And very easy to pierce they were*
> *As they pattered over the lumber there*
> *And rode on two little sacred feet.*
>
> *But alas, on a hill between earth and heaven*
> *One day two nails in a cross were driven,*
> *And fastened it firm to the sacred feet*
> *Where once rode two little sandals sweet;*
> *And Christ and His Mother looked off in death*

*Afar — to the valley of Nazareth*
*Where the carpenter shop was spread with dust*
*And the little blue nails, all packed in rust,*
*Slept in a box on the windowsill,*
*And Joseph lay sleeping under the hill.[52]*

And what does the Carpenter do now that the carpenters will no longer permit Him to carpenter? He becomes a sower and fulfills the parable that He once told: "And behold, the sower went forth to sow."[53] He who had once sowed the blue firmament with stars and the fields with wildflowers, now continues to sow, but with seed of a different kind. His feet are nailed, and yet not even steel stills the progress of His sowing. His feet are dug, and yet He casts the seed to the winds, and the seed is His Blood, each precious drop of it a grain falling to the ground, each sufficient to spring forth into life everlasting.

It is only the soil that differs. There was no one on Calvary that day who did not carry away in his heart the seed of life or death. There never has been and there never will be a creature who, when the last sheaf is bound and the last load garnered, will not be found to have accepted or refused that seed of life, and in doing so, to have signed the warrant of his own destiny.

But the Sower went on sowing His seed, and as He sowed "some fell by the wayside . . . and other some fell upon stony ground, where they had not much earth . . . and others fell among thorns, and the thorns grew up and choked them."[54]

It was everywhere the same seed that fell with the same rich redness, the same beautiful promise of life. It was the soil that was

[52] Leonard Feeney, S.J.
[53] Matt. 13:3.
[54] Matt. 13:4-5, 7.

different. The seed was the redemptive Blood of Christ. The wayside soil was the self-wise group, such as the judges who put Christ to death; men who were walking the ways of men, rather than the ways of God; men who followed the public opinion of the streets, rather than the faith of the hidden Christ. The stony ground was the ignorant group, such as His executioners; men with cold, rocky, unplowed, rough, and uncouth hearts. The thorny soil was the weak group, such as the timid Apostles and disciples, who were off at the border of the crowd, fearful of the thorns of human respect and the shame that is the heritage of the Cross.

&#8252;

### To save us, Christ had to sacrifice Himself

But as He sows, nature changes her complexion. Now, a midnight sky at noon . . . flashes of lightning, like daggers of light . . . demoniac laughter . . . the sob of a woman . . . the sound of a hammer . . . a sigh of pain . . . blasphemies and curses . . . the warbling of a distant bird . . . the lengthening shadow of the Cross . . . audible blood dripping. He saw them as He sowed. They had eyes shifting, doubting, with wicked light; eyes through which Hell itself was looking. They had lips — fierce, fastened, open lips, craters of hate, volcanoes of blasphemy. They had hands — hands that picked up stones, and now hands that opened the granary of His precious side. They had faces — mad, laughing faces, faces that flashed ferocity, faces that came out of the lairs and dens of festering ignorance and crime, faces jeering and roaring about the Cross. And the words they hurled at the Man on the Cross were words in which their consuming envy expressed their argument and their triumph! "Others He saved; Himself He cannot save."[55]

---

[55] Mark 15:31.

They can admit this now, seeing that He is not saving Himself. They can now admit that He saved the son of the widow of Naim. They can now admit that He made the blind to see and the deaf to hear, and even Lazarus to come from his grave. They can now fully avow that He could save others, because now He cannot save Himself.

When He should now put forth His power by coming down from the Cross, by changing a crown of thorns into flowers and nails into rosebuds, He does not. It is only because He is weak. His omnipotence is plain, His feebleness apparent. And as the great flame of love burns itself out, there echoes out over the rocks of Calvary, out even over the hills of Zion, the cry of their hate, the cry of their apparent triumph, the cry of their final victory: "Others He saved; Himself He cannot save!"

Of course He cannot! No man can save himself who saves another. Sacrifice is not weakness, but the obedience to a law, and the law is that if any man will save others, in any salvation whatsoever, the mandate he must obey, the stern condition he must fulfill, the lot he must accept is that he cannot save himself. Such is the paradox of salvation!

Falling leaves cannot save themselves if they are to enrich the soil. The falling acorn cannot save itself if it is to bud a tree. A caterpillar must forfeit its life if it is to become a butterfly. A plant cannot save itself if it is to nourish an animal. An animal cannot save itself if it is to become food for man. A mother cannot save herself if she wishes to save the life of her child. The soldier cannot save himself if he wishes to save his country, nor can the shepherd save himself if he would save his sheep. Christ is the Good Shepherd, and hence, when Jesus would consummate the great salvation, there was no other way to save humanity than to lose Himself, no other way to save us than to lay down His life for our salvation. For to love is never to think of oneself, but to give oneself for the one loved.

But the tragic part of it all was the perversity on the part of human nature, which Christ so tenderly loved and for which He was baptized with the baptism of blood. I say the perversity of mankind, for He who brought salvation to all nations was put to death by His own people. He who taught love for enemies was killed by His friends. He who offered His life was put to death. He who came to save others was crucified by those whom He saved. He who called Himself the seed verified the law of the seed by making death the condition of birth. He who said He had life in abundance was one day apparently to have none of it. He who told the parable of the Good Shepherd who did not flee when he saw the wolf coming, now actually lays down His life for His sheep. Others He saved; Himself He cannot save!

Could not Christ have saved us without the shedding of His Precious Blood? Might He not have sat, like the Greek teachers before Him, in some porch or garden, where the enterprise and intelligence of the world might have sought and found the wisdom that would save it? Might He not, like another Gotama, have sat under a Bodhi tree, and in a moment of illumination have become the Buddha? Might He not, like another Solomon, have installed Himself in a palace of luxury, where refinement, power, and ease would have brought all the nations to His feet?

If He had been only a teacher, a world philosopher, He might have done these things. But He had a deeper work to do. He came not only to teach, but also to save. He had to force the human conscience to stand face-to-face with the sternest, most unwelcome sides of truth, ere He disclosed His divine remedy; and as long as the conditions of life were to stay unchanged, He had to save others by losing Himself. Others He saved; Himself He cannot save!

# God's World and Our Place in It

❧

*We must lose ourselves to follow Christ*

But the servant is not above the Master. The law of the life of Christ must be the law of the life of Christians. If our soul is to be saved for eternity, it must be lost to time. If it is to be saved to the Father's heavenly Mansion, it must be lost to time's poor, dumb show. If it is to be saved for the treasures that rust does not consume, it must be lost to the riches of the world. If it is to be saved for Heaven, it must be lost to earth, for all this is but the continuation of that law of redemption that no one can save himself if he is saving someone else.

To the early martyrs the world said, "You cannot save your bodies if you hold that the love of God is higher than the love of Caesar." Of course they could not save their bodies; it was because they were saving their souls.

To the cloistered orders of our day the world says, "You cannot save yourself for the pleasures and luxuries of the world if you follow the Christian law of penance and sacrifice." Of course they cannot; it is because they are saving the world.

To all the faithful following the morality of Christ, the world will say, "You cannot save yourself for our social life if you deny divorce." Of course they cannot; it is because they are saving themselves for eternal life.

To the Church the world says, "You cannot save yourself for the good opinion of this age, for its easy morality and its broadmindedness, if you oppose it in the name of the unchanging principles of Christ." Of course she cannot save herself for this age; it is because she is saving herself for an age when this age is dead and gone.

Chapter Fifteen

❧

# Surrender leads to true victory

꩜

The time is sunset — that dread day when at high noon the sun hid its light at the passing of Light. The holy body that was purpled with blood from the precious wardrobe of His side, was now at death, laid in a stranger's grave, as at birth it was cradled in a stranger's cave. The rocks, which but a few hours before were shattered by the dripping of His red blood, now have gained a seeming victory by sealing in death the One who said that from rocks He could raise up children to Abraham.[56]

In the last rays of that setting sun, which, like a eucharistic Host, was tabernacled in the flaming monstrance of the west, picture three men, a Hebrew, a Roman, and a Greek, passing before the grave of the One who went down to defeat and stumbling upon the crude board nailed above the Cross that very afternoon. Each dimly reads in his own language the inscription "Jesus of Nazareth, King of the Jews."

The variety of languages, symbols of a variety of nationalities, provokes them to discuss what seems to them an important problem — namely, what will be the most civilizing world influence in fifty years?

[56] Cf. Matt. 3:9.

## God's World and Our Place in It

The Hebrew says the most civilizing world influence in fifty years will be the temple of Jerusalem, from which will radiate under the inspiration of Abraham, Isaac, and Jacob, the religion that will conquer the hearts of the gentile nations and make of the Holy City the Mecca of the world. The Roman contends that within fifty years, the most potent social factor will be the city of Rome, destined to be eternal because it was founded by Romulus and Remus, who in their infancy were nourished by something nonhuman — namely, a wolf, which gave them their extraordinary force and their might. Finally, the Greek, disagreeing with both, argues that in the specified time, the most important world influence will be the wisdom of the Grecian philosophers and their unknown god, to whom a statue, made by human hands, was erected in the marketplace of the great Athens.

Not one of the three gave a thought to the Man who went down to the defeat of the Cross on that Good Friday afternoon. For the Hebrew with his love for religion, and the Roman with his love for law, and the Greek with his love for philosophy, there was not the faintest suggestion that He who called Himself the Way of religion, the Truth of law, and the Light of philosophy, and who was now imprisoned by rock-ribbed earth, would ever again stir the hearts and minds and souls of men. They could not agree upon what would most influence the world in the next generation, but they were all agreed that He whose blood dried upon the Cross that afternoon would never influence it.

And yet, ere the sun had risen on that third day, in that springtime when all dead things were coming to life, He who had laid down His life took it up again and walked into the garden in the glory of the new Easter morning. Ere the fishermen disciples had gone back to their nets and their boats on the Sea of Galilee, He who had announced His own birth to a Virgin now told a penitent harlot to tell Peter that the sign of Jonah had been fulfilled. Long before nature could heal hideous scars on hands and feet and side, nature herself was to have the only serious wound she ever received — namely, the empty tomb, as He was seen walking on the day of triumph with five wounds gleaming as five great suns, as an eternal proof that love is stronger than death.

Fifty years passed, and what happened? Within that time, the army of Titus struck the Temple of Jerusalem and left not a stone on stone, while over the empty tomb all the nations of the earth saw a new spiritual edifice arise, whose cornerstone was that which the builders rejected. Within fifty years, Rome discovered the real reason for its immortality; it was not because Romulus and Remus, nourished by the wolf, had come to dwell there, but because the spiritual Romulus and Remus, Peter and Paul, nourished on the Bread descended from Heaven, came there to preach the eternal love of the risen Christ. Within fifty years, the dominant spiritual force in Greece was not the unknown god made by human hands, but the God whom St. Paul announced to the Areopagites when, stretching forth his hands he said: "I found an altar on which was written: 'To the Unknown God.' What, therefore, you worship without knowing it, I therefore preach to you: God, who made the world and all things therein . . . for in Him we live and move and are."[57]

Fifty years passed, and Jerusalem would have been forgotten, had not Jesus died there. Rome would have perished, had not a fisherman died there. Athens would have been forgotten, had not the risen Christ been preached there. Fifty years passed, and the three cultures in which He was crucified now sang His name in praise. The Cross, which was the instrument of shame, became the

[57] Acts 17:23-24, 28.

badge of honor, as Calvary was renewed on Christian altars in the language of Hebrew, Latin, and Greek.

⚓

*Christ turned defeat into victory*

The world was wrong, and Christ was right. He who had the power to lay down His life had the power to take it up again. He who willed to be born, willed to die. And He who knew how to die knew also how to be reborn and to give to this poor tiny planet of ours an honor and a glory that flaming suns and jealous planets do not share: the glory of one forsaken grave.

The great lesson of Easter Day is that a Victor may be judged from a double point of view: that of the world and that of God. From the world's point of view, Christ failed on Good Friday. From God's point of view, Christ had won. Those who put Him to death gave Him the very chance He required; those who closed the door of the sepulcher gave Him the very door that He desired to fling open; their seeming triumph led to His greatest victory.

Christmas told the story that Divinity is always where the world least expects to find it, for no one expected to see Divinity wrapped in swaddling clothes and laid in a manger. Easter repeats that Divinity is always where the world least expects to find it, for no one in the world expected that a defeated man would be a victor, that the rejected cornerstone would be the head of the building, that the dead would walk, and that He who was ignored in a tomb should be our Resurrection and our Life.

And so on Easter Day, I sing, not the song of the victors, but of those who go down to defeat:

> *I sing the hymn of the conquered,*
> *who fall in the Battle of Life,*

*The hymn of the wounded, the beaten,*
*who died overwhelmed in the strife;*
*Not the jubilant song of the victors,*
*for whom the resounding acclaim*
*Of nations was lifted in chorus,*
*whose brows wear the chaplet of fame,*
*But the hymn of the low and the humble,*
*the weary, the broken in heart,*
*Who strove and who failed, acting bravely*
*a silent and desperate part,*
*Whose youth bore no flower in its branches,*
*whose hopes burned in ashes away,*
*From whose hands slipped the prize they*
*had grasped at, who stood at the dying of day*
*With the wreck of their life all around them,*
*unpitied, unheeded, alone,*
*With death swooping down o'er their failure,*
*and all but their faith overthrown.*
*While the voice of the world shouts its chorus —*
*its paean for those who have won*
*While the trumpet is sounding triumphant,*
*and high to the breeze and the sun*
*Glad banners are waving, hands*
*clapping, and hurrying feet*
*Thronging after the laurel-crowned victors,*
*I stand on the field of defeat,*
*In the shadow, with those who are fallen,*
*and wounded, and dying, and there*
*Chant a requiem low, place my hand on their*
*pain-knotted brows, breathe a prayer,*
*Hold the hand that is helpless, and whisper,*

> *"They only the victory win,*
> *Who have fought the good fight, and have*
> *vanquished the demon that tempts from within;*
> *Who have held to their faith unseduced by the*
> *prize that the world holds on high;*
> *Who have dared for a high cause to suffer,*
> *resist, fight, if need be, to die."*
> *Speak, History! Who are Life's victors?*
> *Unroll thy long annals and say,*
> *Are they these whom the world called the victors,*
> *who won the success of a day?*
> *The martyrs or Nero? The Spartans,*
> *who fell at Thermopylae's tryst?*
> *Or the Persians and Xerxes? His judges*
> *or Socrates? Pilate or Christ?*

Unroll the scrolls of time, and see how the lesson of that first Easter is repeated as each new Easter tells the story of the great Captain, who found His way out of the grave and revealed that lasting victory must always mean defeat in the eyes of the world. At least a dozen times in her life of twenty centuries, the world in the first flush of its momentary triumph sealed the tomb of the Church, set her watch and left her as a dead, breathless, and defeated thing, only to see her rising from the grave and walking in the victory of her new Easter morn.

In the first few centuries, thousands upon thousands of Christians crimsoned the sands of the Coliseum with their blood in testimony to their Faith. In the eyes of the world, Caesar was victor and the martyrs were defeated. Yet in that very generation, while pagan Rome with her brazen and golden trumpets proclaimed to the four corners of the earth her victory over the defeated Christ — "Where there is Caesar, there is power" — there swept from out of the catacombs and deserted places, like their leader from the grave, the conquering army chanting its song of victory: "Wherever there is Christ, there is life."

Who today knows the names of Rome's executioners? But who does not know the names of Rome's martyrs? Who today recalls with pride the deeds of a Nero or a Diocletian? But who does not venerate the heroism and sanctity of an Agnes or a Cecilia? And so, on Easter Day, I sing, not the song of the victors, but of those who go down to defeat.

Come now closer to our own times, to the last quarter of the nineteenth century. During those days, France was celebrating its great victory over the Church in a wave of anticlericalism that made it a shame and scandal to be a follower of Christ. There was hardly a lip of the world that did not pronounce in praise, and hardly an ear that did not hear in joy, the names of Jules Steeg of Parliament and Ferdinand Buisson, the Minister of State, the two men most responsible for the seeming victory over the Church.

At that very time, in a little city a few hours outside of Paris, a young girl hidden away in the shadow of the cloister was pouring out her prayerful life for Christ and, like her Master, going down to defeat in the eyes of the sinful world. On this Easter Day, who in this country, who even in France ever mentions the names or remembers the deeds of a Steeg or a Buisson? But who does not know of the Little Flower, Thérèse of Lisieux? She who was defeated in the eyes of the world is the victor in the eyes of God, and so on Easter Day I sing, not the song of the victors, but of those who go down to defeat.

Finally the Easter lesson comes to our own lives. It has been suggested that it is better to go down to defeat in the eyes of the world by accepting the voice of conscience rather than to win the victory of a false public opinion; that it is better to go down to defeat in the sanctity of the marriage bond than to win the passing victory of divorce; that it is better to go down to defeat in the fruit of love than to win the passing victory of a barren union; that it is better to go down to defeat in the love of the Cross than to win the passing victory of a world that crucifies. And now it is suggested in conclusion that it is better to go down to defeat in the eyes of the world by giving to God that which is wholly and totally ours.

❖

### God desires our will

If we give God our energy, we give Him back His own gift. If we give Him our talents, our joys, and our possessions, we return to Him that which He placed into our hands, not as owners, but as mere trustees. There is only one thing in the world that we can call our own. There is only one thing we can give to God that is ours as against His, which not even He will take away, and that is our own will, with its power to choose the object of its love.

Hence, the most perfect gift we can give to God is the gift of our will. The giving of that gift to God is the greatest defeat that we can suffer in the eyes of the world, but it is the greatest victory we can win in the eyes of God. In surrendering it, we seem to lose everything, yet defeat is the seed of victory, as the diamond is the child of night. The giving of our will is the recovery of all our will ever sought: the perfect Life, the perfect Truth, and the perfect Love which is God! And so on Easter Day, sing, not the song of the victors, but of those who go down to defeat.

What care we if the road of this life is steep, if the poverty of Bethlehem, the loneliness of Galilee, and the sorrow of the Cross are ours? Fighting under the holy inspiration of One who has conquered the world, why should we shrink from letting the broad stroke of our challenge ring out on the shield of the world's hypocrisy? Why should we be afraid to draw the sword and let its first stroke be the slaying of our own selfishness? Marching under the leadership of the Captain of the Five Scars, fortified by His sacraments, strengthened by His infallible truth, divinized by His redemptive love, we need never fear the outcome of the battle of life. We need never doubt the issue of the only struggle that matters. We need never ask whether we will win or lose. Why, we have already won — only the news has not yet leaked out!

Biographical Note

# Fulton J. Sheen
(1895-1979)

Pope John Paul II once said to Fulton Sheen, "You have written and spoken well of the Lord Jesus." But the popular priest whom millions watched weekly on television had a more humble view of himself: "The Lord once used an ass to ride to Jerusalem. Now He uses an ass on TV." In his witty way, he recognized himself as an instrument of Christ.

Fulton John Sheen was born in El Paso, Illinois, in 1895. Even as a child, he prized education. In high school, he won a three-year university scholarship, but, on the advice of a priest, he turned it down to pursue a vocation to the priesthood.

He attended St. Viator College and Seminary in Bourbannais, Illinois, and studied further at St. Paul Seminary in St. Paul, Minnesota. In 1919, he was ordained a priest for the Diocese of Peoria. He earned a Licentiate in Sacred Theology and a Bachelor of Canon Law at the Catholic University of America and a Doctorate at Catholic University of Louvain, Belgium. In his studies, Sheen sought to learn two things: "First, what the modern world is thinking about; second, how to answer the errors of modern philosophy in the light of the philosophy of St. Thomas."

Indeed St. Thomas Aquinas influenced him greatly. Sheen's goal was to "make St. Thomas functional, not for a school, but for a world . . . a remedy against the anarchy of ideas, riot of philosophical systems, and breakdown of spiritual forces."

Sheen received numerous teaching offers, but turned them down in obedience to his bishop and became an assistant pastor in a rural parish. Having thus tested his obedience, the bishop later permitted him to teach at Catholic University of America and at St. Edmund's College, Ware, England, where he met another individual who influenced him: G. K. Chesterton, whose weekly BBC radio broadcast inspired Sheen's later NBC broadcast "The Catholic Hour" (1930-1952).

In 1952, Sheen began appearing on ABC in his own series, "Life Is Worth Living." Despite being given a time slot that forced him to compete with Milton Berle and Frank Sinatra, the dynamic Sheen enjoyed enormous success and in 1954 reached twenty-five million viewers — non-Catholics as well as Catholics. He designed his presentations for viewers of all faiths and backgrounds and covered a wide range of topics.

His weekly television program made Sheen one of this country's most well-known priests. But even off the screen he was winning souls for Christ. His courses attracted people from diverse backgrounds, and his powerful, eloquent preaching drew many to the Faith. When asked by Pope Pius XII how many converts he had made, Sheen responded, "Your Holiness, I have never counted them. I am always afraid if I did count them, I might think I made them, instead of the Lord."

He gave annual Good Friday homilies at New York's St. Patrick's Cathedral, gave numerous retreats for priests and religious, and preached at summer conferences in Cambridge, England and London's Westminster Cathedral. In 1948, he accompanied Cardinal Spellman on a forty-day Pacific Tour, during which he preached more than two hundred times.

"If you want people to stay as they are," Sheen said, "tell them what they want to hear. If you want to improve them, tell them what they should know." This he did, not only in his preaching, but also in the more than ninety books he wrote. His *Peace of Soul* was sixth on the *New York Times'* bestseller list.

Sheen served as Bishop of Rochester, New York (1966-1969) and Auxiliary Bishop of New York (1951-1966). While he was National Director of the Society for the Propagation of the Faith (SPF), the Church's overseas mission, to which he donated what he was paid for his television appearances, donations to the SPF soared. Sheen traveled to Catholic missions in other countries and founded and edited *Mission* magazine to reveal the plight of the poor throughout the world. He served on the Commission on the Missions at Vatican II and in 1969 was appointed by Pope Paul VI to the Papal Commission for Nonbelievers and named Titular Archbishop of Newport, Wales.

Sheen's two great loves were for the Blessed Mother and for the Eucharist. He made a daily holy hour in front of the Blessed Sacrament, from which he drew strength and inspiration to preach the gospel and in the presence of which he prepared his homilies. "I beg [Christ] every day to keep me strong physically and alert mentally in order to preach His gospel and proclaim His Cross and Resurrection," he said. "I am so happy doing this that I sometimes feel that when I come to the good Lord in Heaven, I will take a few days' rest and then ask Him to allow me to come back again to this earth to do some more work."

The good Lord called Fulton J. Sheen home in 1979. His television broadcasts, now on tape, and his books continue his earthly work of winning souls for Christ. Sheen's cause for canonization has been opened in Rome.

Sophia Institute® is a nonprofit institution that seeks to restore man's knowledge of eternal truth, including man's knowledge of his own nature, his relation to other persons, and his relation to God. Sophia Institute Press® serves this end in numerous ways: it publishes translations of foreign works to make them accessible to English-speaking readers; it brings out-of-print books back into print; and it publishes important new books that fulfill the ideals of Sophia Institute®. These books afford readers a rich source of the enduring wisdom of mankind. Sophia Institute Press® makes these high-quality books available to the general public by using advanced technology and by soliciting donations to subsidize its general publishing costs. Your generosity can help Sophia Institute Press® to provide the public with editions of works containing the enduring wisdom of the ages. Please send your tax-deductible contribution to the address below.

*For your free catalog, call:*

**Toll-free: 1-800-888-9344**

Sophia Institute Press® • Box 5284 • Manchester, NH 03108
www.sophiainstitute.com

Sophia Institute® is a tax-exempt institution as defined by the Internal Revenue Code, Section 501(c)(3). Tax I.D. 22-2548708.